COMMUNION WITH GOD

Robert Philip (1791-1858)

COMMUNION WITH GOD

A GUIDE TO THE DEVOTIONAL SPIRIT

BY ROBERT PHILIP

REFORMATION HERITAGE BOOKS
Grand Rapids, Michigan

Copyright © 2006
Reformation Heritage Books
2965 Leonard St., NE
Grand Rapids, MI 49525
616-977-0599 / Fax 616-285-3246
e-mail: orders@heritagebooks.org
website: www.heritagebooks.org

ISBN #1-892777-46-0
#978-1-892777-46-1

Reprinted from the seventh edition
George Philip & Son, London, England

*For additional Reformed literature, both new and used,
request a free book list from the above address.*

BIOGRAPHICAL FOREWORD

The books of Robert Philip were very popular in nineteenth-century Great Britain and America for their practical guidance on promoting personal, Reformed piety. A biblical, heart-warming spirituality glowed from their pages; the reader's attention was drawn to God's storehouse of divine comforts. Today, Philip has become relatively unknown, and his works have faded into obscurity. This book is the first effort to bring Philip's marvelous writings back to light.

Robert Philip was born in Huntly, Aberdeenshire, Scotland, in May of 1791. His father was an elder in a Congregational church pastored by George Cowie, well-known as "the Whitefield of northern Scotland." Young Robert grew up in a vibrant, evangelistic church of Puritan persuasion and in the company of some of the most important leaders of Independency in Scotland. After his father's death in 1806, he moved to Aberdeen, where he acquired a job as a clerk and became a member of the Belmont Congregational Church. His pastor there, Dr. John Philip (no relation), encouraged him to pursue gospel ministry, and provided him preparatory studies before entering more formal training.

In 1811, Robert Philip began his theological studies at Hoxton Academy in London, under the guidance of its president, Dr. Robert Simpson, known as "a man of God mighty in prayer." Philip assumed his first pastorate in 1815 for the Newbington Chapel in Liverpool. His labors there were characterized by an intense desire to be "made all things to all men," so that he "might by all means save some" (1 Cor. 9:22). Being a port town, Liverpool was an ideal place for ministry to sailors. Philip recognized the neglect shown to this class of men, and made it his mission to reach them with the gospel. He familiarized himself with seafaring events in order to gain their respect, and published a series of his addresses to sailors as *The Bethel Flag; or, Sermons to Seamen.*

Meanwhile, in 1818, Philip married Hannah Lassel of Bolton, Lancashire. In 1826, the Philips moved to London, where Robert Philip spent the next thirty years as minister of Maberly Chapel. Here he often preached up to four times on a Sunday, twice in his own congregation and once or twice elsewhere. He developed a greater focus on experiential Christianity and piety, which he found to be more effective in building up a healthy church than his earlier efforts.

Philip authored a series of *Experimental Guides* and two series of books intended for young men and women, eventually collected under the titles *The Young Man's Closet Library* and *The Young Lady's Closet Library*, all of which promoted a healthy spirituality among evangelical Christians through simple, earnest, and practical writing. He also produced works on Richard Baxter, George Whitefield, John Bunyan, William Milne, and John Campbell, which gave Christian biography a devotional turn. One of Philip's final and most helpful books, *The Eternal; or, the God of Our Fathers,* was the outgrowth of a series of Sunday morning sermons on the attributes of God. In all of these books, Philip demonstrates a great indebtedness to the Puritans and a drive to see their experiential Christianity flourish in the context of his own day.

Tributes to Philip's writing came from many quarters, including the *British Quarterly Review, Literary World, Christian Age, Eclectic Review, Evangelical Magazine, Sword and Trowel,* and *Glasgow Herald.* The *Edinburgh Daily Review* wrote, "His style is clear and

earnest, and his thoughts always practical in their bearing....
They display great beauty and tenderness of composition." The
American Literary Advocate claimed that "no modern theological
works are so widely circulated amongst all denominations in
America as Mr. Philip's."

Philip also dedicated himself to the promotion of foreign
missions. He was especially drawn to China, and took several
trips there on behalf of the London Missionary Society, of
which he was eventually made director.

The early 1850s marked a decline in Philip's activity. After
receiving an honorary doctorate of divinity from Dartmouth
College in 1852, which was a significant recognition of his
influence in the United States, Philip's work became confined
to his pastoral duties. His health grew increasingly worse, leading him to resign from the pastorate at Maberly Chapel in
1855. He died at his home on May 1, 1858, and was buried in
Abney Park cemetery.

Although written generations ago, we hope that Philip's
books will be used by God for a renewal of experiential
Christianity in our day. In this reprint, *Communion with God: A
Guide to the Devotional Spirit*, Philip underscores the importance
of appreciating and utilizing the believer's gracious access to
God; he aims to cultivate a devotional spirit among the people
of God so that their joy may be full. He brings tender encouragement to the faint of heart, yet assures the presumptuous
that holiness is essential to true fellowship with God. Whether
you are seeking to lay hold of God's promises, struggling with
assurance, enduring trials, lacking zeal, or simply desiring further encouragement in your prayer life, reading Philip's
Communion with God prayerfully will be a blessing to your soul
and a sure "guide to the devotional spirit."

— Joel Beeke and Jay Collier

CONTENTS

COMMUNION WITH GOD.

CHAPTER I.

ACCESS TO GOD.

THE highest human honour is access to the king. Even a single interview with the monarch is generally coveted, and if obtained never forgotten. How much more should access to the "King Eternal, Immortal, and Invisible," be prized and improved! But, alas! it is not so in general. We are naturally averse to "draw nigh unto God." The human mind, whilst unaffected by eternal things, regards prayer rather as an irksome task than as a glorious privilege. Accordingly, we invent or avail ourselves of excuses for the neglect of prayer, and are not often very sorry when kept or called away from the throne of grace. Even when bowing before it in secret, and whilst no external objects distract or divert our minds, we are prone to hurry over devotion, and but too willing to return to the world. The social circle or a favourite book has, in general, greater charms for us, and can detain us much longer than the mercy-seat of God. We find it easier to come down from the closet to the parlour, than to go up from the parlour to the closet. "The hour of prayer" is far less punctually kept than the hour of any secular or social engagement. The time which ought to be sacred to God is often sacrificed to the world; but we seldom sacrifice to God any of the time which belongs to the world. In a word, there is nothing we have more reason to be ashamed of than our low views, and our lower feelings upon the subject of secret prayer.

And yet prayer is access to God, and may be communion with God. It may be to us what praise is to angels and glorified spirits—"fellowship with God and the Lamb." We may come as near to the Eternal Mind in prayer, as they come to the eternal throne in praise. What then ought we to think of our *reluctance* to pray? Were any angel or spirit in heaven half as reluctant to sing the new song, or to lay his crown at the feet of the Lamb, we should condemn him at once, and expect his expulsion from heaven. We should no more think of excusing or palliating his conduct, than that of "the angels who kept not their first estate;" nor would his imprisonment in their chains of darkness, nor his impalement in their penal fires, surprise us. Thus promptly and justly do we judge in the case of those who have "access" to God in heaven. We expect them to

" serve Him without weariness." Let not the impression of this supposed case be defeated by the fact,
that the spirits in heaven have nothing else to do.
The difference between their lot and our own is,
indeed, immense. They have no cares, nor corrup-
tions, nor temptations, to hinder or harass them ; but

> " What various hindrances we meet
> In coming to the mercy-seat ! "

True ; and just because they are many and great,
the greater need we have for coming often and
regularly, that we may obtain mercy and find grace
to help. For if glorified spirits could neither be
happy nor safe without communion with God, how
much less can we be happy without it in a world so
trying, or safe in a world so ensnaring. They need
communion with God in order to sustain their " eternal
weight of glory ;" how much more do we need it in
order to sustain our patience under afflictions, and
our character amidst temptations.

It will assist us still farther in forming a just judgment of our own hearts and habits, if we review some
of the instances of special " access " to God, which
have been vouchsafed " at sundry times and in divers
manners to the fathers." Under the law, the high
priest had access annually to the mercy-seat in the
holy of holies ; and when within the vail God com-
muned with him from between the cherubim. He
could say with certainty as he entered with blood and
incense, " I will hear what God the Lord will speak

for He will speak peace to His people." Now, with such an introduction as the typical blood of atonement, and such a welcome awaiting him, what should we have thought and said of the high priest if he had neglected to go into the holy of holies, or had not gone up to the mercy-seat, or had come out before he heard what God the Lord would speak? Had any priest been guilty of this neglect, all hearts would have been shocked at his impiety, and all voices united in condemning him. We should have expected to hear that, like the offerers of " strange fire," he was suddenly and signally consumed by penal fire. You feel this through all your soul, and are glad that there is no instance of a high priest neglecting to draw nigh to God when within the vail. But is it not more shocking and sinful not to draw nigh to God, now that the eternal throne is the mercy-seat, and the blood of the Lamb our introduction and plea? That precious " blood " is both the plea for, and the pledge of, our success in prayer. And access to God on the mercy-seat is now daily. At all times, in all places, and under all circumstances, we may " come boldly to the throne of grace to obtain mercy, and find grace to help in time of need." Why, then, is this freedom of access so little prized or improved? We cannot say that it is less interesting to enter our closets to commune with God, than it was to enter the holy of holies. The scene is, indeed, less impressive in its external circumstances, and it makes no appeal to our senses ; but when it is duly examined it is really more useful than all the glories of the holy of holies. The ark of the covenant was, no doubt, splendid; and the golden mercy-seat sublime, and the cherubim majestic; and the cloud of glory crowning the whole effulgent; but the whole were only "shadows of good things to come;" whereas we have in our closets the "good things" themselves. There we may behold the brightness of the Father's glory in the face of Jesus, and see in His person and work the substance of all that was shadowed within the vail, and more than all that was typified throughout the temple. Our perfect and preserved BIBLE is itself more wonderful and glorious than "the cloud of glory." That Shekinah of the Divine presence was, even when its radiance "filled the temple," a *dark* cloud, compared with the light which is embodied in and shines from the sun of Scripture. Possessing this great and true light, we have no need to regret the loss of anything which the ancient temple contained; for this light shows God to *be* all, and to be *doing* all upon the throne of grace in heaven, that He was and did upon the mercy-seat on earth. If, indeed, God had become less accessible, less sympathising, or less faithful in reference to prayer than He was in the temple, there would be reason to regret our transfer from the temple to the *closet;* but as God himself is the same for ever—His heart the same in kindness—His hand the same in bounty and power—the changes of place and circumstances are of no consequence whatever. All the real value of the holy of holies and its magnificent mercy-seat was, that there **God** heard and answered prayer. But for that, and what they typified of Christ, they would have been mere gorgeous ornaments; and as types are now useless, and the answer of prayer secured by the intercession of Christ, the "closet" is preferable to the temple, if communion with God be our object. For in the "closet" God is "ALL in ALL." When we retire to it we meet God only, we speak to God alone.

ALONE with God! How solemn and sublime! Such access to Him has no parallel in heaven itself. It is as if all the spirits around the eternal throne were moved back to "the borders of Immanuel's land," whenever a new spirit was about to enter, that thus its first interview might be with God alone, and its first emotions seen only by Him. Drawing nigh to God in the closet has all the *secrecy*, and none of the overwhelming solemnity, of such an interview.

The soul is there with God alone, as if it alone engaged all His notice. It has God wholly to itself; and may unbosom and plead as if He had no one else to attend unto at the moment.

We could not have entered within the vail of the temple, even if we had lived when the temple was in all its glory; but, if we could have entered to pray before the mercy-seat, what would it have been compared with thus meeting in the "closet" with nothing but God, and with God all to ourselves? Oh! why should we ever be reluctant to pray, or heartless in prayer? Secret prayer is a private interview with

God, as real as that at the bush in Midian, or that on mount Peniel, vouchsafed to Moses and Jacob. If, therefore, we would readily welcome such visits from God as the patriarchs were favoured with, and would consider even one visit to be, on His part, an act of infinite condescension, what ought we to think of the daily privilege of visiting God in secret, and being noticed, heard, and remembered by Him for good? Do consider: in the "closet" we are allowed to say all unto God that we could wish to say if we were praying upon the very spot where archangels adore, and redeemed spirits sing. There is no note on the harp of Gabriel more welcome to Jehovah than the cry of a penitent for mercy, or the supplication of a child for grace. God makes it even a *condition* of coming to Him, that "we believe that He is the rewarder of them who diligently seek Him." Think of all the armies of heaven rolling from their harps the anthems of eternity. Are they noticed and approved? Hear, then, the voice of God outspeaking the chorus of heaven! "Thus saith the High and Holy One, who inhabiteth eternity, Unto that man will I look, and with that man will I dwell, who is of a contrite spirit, and who trembleth at my word." Truly, prayer is "access to God!" He dwells with the prayerful, as He inhabits eternity,—actually, willingly, and with delight. How willingly and cheerfully, therefore, ought we to enter into our closets, and pray to the Father who seeth in secret, and rewardeth openly! Oh, had JOB known all this as clearly as we do, how would he have prized and improved such access and welcome to God! He would not have grudged the time, nor shrunk from the effort, required in drawing nigh to God. When he exclaimed—" Oh! that I knew where I might find Him, that I might come even to His seat!" he would have gladly gone anywhere to find God. If "His seat" had been on the loftiest and coldest summit of Lebanon, and Lebanon quaking like Sinai, Job would have climbed to it, to meet God in mercy. If "His seat" had been in the depths of the most desolate wilderness, or at the uttermost parts of the sea, Job would have travelled to it willingly, to " order his cause before God." We feel sure of this ; it being so consistent with the patriarch's character. Indeed, we should have readily blamed him, in the upbraiding spirit of his three friends, if he had been unwilling to go anywhere to find God. Well, we know where to find God.

"We have no such lengths to go ;"

no such questions to ask. We know where He " waiteth to be gracious." God is always to be found at our own HOME, when we seek Him with the whole heart. More intimate communion may be found with Him in the closet at home, than was found in the ancient temple, even by those who travelled from Dan and Beersheba to appear before God in Zion. They could not enter into the holy place made with hands, but had to worship afar off; "for the Law made nothing perfect ; but the bringing in of a better

hope did : by the which we draw nigh unto God."
Well, therefore, might Paul add, " Having, therefore,
brethren, boldness *(freedom)* to enter into the holiest
by the blood of Jesus, by a new and living way,
which He hath consecrated for us, through the vail ;
and having an High Priest over the house of God, let
us draw near with a true heart, in full assurance of
faith." Thus it is, that "access" to God is the
pledge of ACCEPTANCE with God. And, until this be
understood and believed, neither the duty nor the
privilege of secret prayer will have much influence
upon our hearts and habits. So long as we have any
doubt, or feel it but a. " peradventure," whether we
shall really " obtain mercy, and find grace," we shall
not come often nor willingly to the throne of grace.
While prayer is at all regarded as hopeless work, it
will continue to be heartless work.

Now, many do doubt very much, whether they
shall succeed in asking for salvation ; and they are
very much confirmed in this habit of doubting, by
observing some who have prayed much and long, but
who are yet, by their own confession, quite uncertain
as to their own acceptance with God. Such persons
are not exactly hopeless, nor do they insinuate anything against the efficacy of prayer ; but they have so
little hope, and that little is so fluctuating, that the
witnesses of it are not much encouraged to pray from
their example. We have felt this, when we have
found some man of prayer a man of fear. And as we
feel and ought to feel, that God might justly refuse to

answer our prayers for salvation; and as we see that He seems in some instances to refuse peace to better men, we are thus led into a suspicion of His willingness to save us. And this doubting habit is still farther confirmed, when our own experince in prayer is similar to that of the persons just described. When we find that but little hope, and no certainty, follows our own prayers, and that we obtain no solid peace or enjoyment, and that the result is still as doubtful as ever, and that we know not what to think of our case, we are thus drawn farther and farther into the wards of Doubting Castle, and away from the throne of grace.

Now, under these circumstances, it is not by splendid descriptions of that "glorious high throne," nor by glowing pictures of the solemnity or sweetness of prayer, nor by strong assertions about angels not being more welcome, nor even by appeals to the success of others; it is not by these things alone, nor chiefly, that we can be charmed back to the throne, or kept near to it. These things have much weight, and a sweet influence upon the mind, whilst the mind can cherish the hope of eventual success; but whilst that is doubted, they will not render us truly devotional. Indeed, we shall never pray much nor with much pleasure until we are persuaded that we shall not pray in vain. Access to God will be prized, just in proportion as we feel sure of acceptance with God.

"Is it, then," it will be said by some, "our *duty* to

believe that we shall find the mercy we pray for?
Are we warranted and bound to calculate upon acceptance with God, when we have sought it with all our
heart and soul?" What saith the Scripture? For
we ought to take no word, but the word of God, on
this subject. Now the Scripture speaketh expressly
on this point : "He that cometh to God MUST believe
that He is the rewarder of them that diligently seek
Him." And again, "Whosoever shall call upon the
name of the Lord SHALL be saved." Thus both the
promise and the precept render it the duty of the
prayerful to believe that "through the grace of our
Lord Jesus Christ" they *shall* be saved. It is by
overlooking this grand fact that so many of the
prayerful are fearful. They watch, indeed, for
answers to their prayer ; but they look unto their own
hearts for them, instead of looking also to the word
of God. This is a grievous mistake. The state of
our hearts should not, indeed, be overlooked ; but,
whilst this is true, it is equally true that our hearts
cannot *feel* what we do not *believe.* If, after praying
fervently for MERCY, we sit down to examine solemnly
whether we feel any hope, peace, or joy, springing up
in our hearts, we ought not to be surprised if we feel
nothing of the kind, so long as our attention is confined to our hearts. The answer to such prayers is
in God's *promises* to the prayerful ; and, therefore,
until they are noticed and believed, we cannot *feel*
that our prayers are answered. It is what God has
written that produces what should be *felt;* and it is

by *believing* what He has promised that hope and peace arise in the mind. Now God has promised that "whosoever shall call upon the name of the Lord shall be saved." If, therefore, we are conscious of having sought, in good earnest, the salvation of God by the blood of the Lamb, and for holy purposes, it is now as much our duty to believe that we shall be saved, as it was our duty to pray for it. Our salvation began, in fact, when we began to seek it with our whole heart; and it will go on, in holiness and happiness, just in proportion as we cultivate devotional habits. Indeed, a devotional spirit is itself one of the chief parts of personal salvation, and both the pledge and prelude of the whole.

It is when these things are understood by the prayerful, that the closet becomes, like the house of God, "the gate of heaven;" and that we obey the call to "enter" it, with something of the same spirit in which we wish to welcome the invitation of the Judge, when He shall say from the great white throne, "Come, ye blessed, inherit the kingdom prepared for you." No one "on the right hand" will refuse or hesitate to enter the "kingdom" then; and no one who believes that access to God is in order to acceptance with God, will refuse to enter the "closet" now. For the *prayerless* do not believe in the efficacy of prayer.

CHAPTER II.

THE PROMISES OF GOD TO THE PRAYERFUL THE
REAL ANSWERS TO PRAYER.

NO complaint is more common amongst one class of those who pray in good earnest for mercy and grace, than that they obtain no *answer* to their prayers. Their strong cries for pardon, although often uttered "with tears," are not followed by a *sense* of pardon. The groanings of their spirit for peace with God, although "unutterable," owing to their depth, are not followed by any calm of conscience. Even their entreaties for some faint gleam of hope, lead to little more than the suppression of absolute despair, and not always to that.

In such cases, it is no wonder that complaints should be uttered, and dejection felt. "Hope deferred maketh the heart sick." It does not, however, harden the heart. Accordingly, the complaints of the disappointed breathe no charge or insinuation against the faithfulness of God, and imply no reflection upon His character. The unsuccessful suppliants lay all the blame upon themselves; and even those of them who resolve their failure into sovereignty, do not impeach the justice of that sovereignty. They feel their own utter unworthiness, and see clearly that they have no personal or legal claim upon the mercy of God; and, under this conviction, all their complaints are deep regrets, and never, in calm moments, murmurings or upbraidings. Whilst they exclaim, with David, "O my God, I cry in the day time, but Thou hearest not; and in the night season, and am not silent." They add with him, "But Thou art holy, O Thou that inhabitest the praises of Israel; I am a worm, and no man." Thus they find, in the holiness of the Divine character, and in the unholiness of their own character, overwhelming and silencing reasons for their want of success in prayer.

Now there is so much real humility in this state of mind, and it is so like the temper of David, and of other true penitents under the Old Covenant, that no minister of the New Covenant would hesitate to encourage such persons. He is not, however, an "*able*" minister of the New Covenant who merely assures them that "delay is not denial," even if he add to that proverb the sacred oracle, "Though the vision tarry, wait for it." There is, indeed, much truth and encouragement, too, in both the proverb and the oracle. In reference to many things pertaining to life and godliness, they can hardly be too often remembered, nor too strictly applied by the prayerful. They are not, however, very applicable, nor intended to apply, to the case of fervent prayer for a *personal interest* in the great salvation. In the matter of hope or peace, there is, happily, neither denial nor delay on the part of God. "He that asketh, receiveth ; and he that seeketh, findeth ;" whether he know it or not at the time. The vision itself does not "tarry," however long and slow the prayerful are in discovering it. The message sent to Daniel, after his fervent prayers, is, in effect, the assurance given to every one who is seriously seeking for mercy and grace through the blood of the Lamb : "Fear not ; for from the first day that thou didst set thine heart to understand, and to chasten thyself before thy God, thy words were heard." In the case of Daniel, an angel, indeed, was the bearer of this assurance ; and in our case, no such messenger is vouchsafed. An apostle of the Lamb, however, assures us, upon the same authority, that "if we ask anything according to His will, God heareth us." John calls this "the confidence" which the prayerful have in God ; and adds, "If we know that He hears us, whatsoever we ask, we know that we have" (or shall have) "the petitions we desired of Him" (1 John v. 14, 15). This is, indeed, strong language, and must seem strange to those who have never duly considered it before. But it is not stronger than, nor at all different from that employed by the Saviour, when He enforced and encouraged secret prayer. "Ask," said Christ, "and it *shall* be given you ; seek, and ye *shall* find ; knock, and it *shall* be opened unto you : for every one that asketh, receiveth ; and he that seeketh, findeth ; and to him that knocketh, it shall be opened" (Matt. vii. 7, 8). In all this we hear nothing, and see nothing that sanctions or suggests the popular notion of *denial* or *delay*.

There are, indeed, instances both of denial and delay to be found in the Scriptures. Paul besought the Lord "thrice," that the thorn in the flesh might be removed from him ; but his request was not complied with. It was not thus, however, that his fervent prayers at Damascus were treated. There, he was praying for his *soul*, and for *salvation;* and, at the end of three days, Ananias was sent to assure him that he had obtained mercy, and found grace. Now this fact is characteristic of God's usual plan in answering prayer. When the blessings prayed for are temporal things, or those spiritual things which belong to the prosperity, rather than to the safety, of the soul, there is often, in the former case, denial ; and in the latter, delay : but when the prayer is, like that of the publican, for *mercy*, the prayerful, like the publican, go down to their "house justified ; for he that humbleth himself shall be exalted" (Matt. xviii. 14). Thus it is that denial, when it occurs in the case of the humble, regards temporal things only ; and delay, when it occurs, is always owing to some defect of their humility. This is one general principle of God's plan of answering prayer. Another is, that, if we regard sin in our hearts, "the Lord will not hear us." Agreeably to this high and holy principle, James explained the unanswered prayers of the Jewish converts: "Ye ask, and receive not, because ye ask amiss, that ye may consume it upon your lusts" (Jas. iv. 3). Whoever, therefore, seeks mercy or grace for unholy, or not for holy, purposes, is sure to be denied. All grace is for gracious purposes; and all mercy to promote holiness. A third principle of God's plan of answering prayer is, that we "*must* believe that He is the rewarder of them who diligently seek Him." Hence, the express and authoritative injunction to every praying man: "Let him ask in faith, nothing wavering;" or, undoubtingly: "for he that wavereth *(doubteth)* is like a wave of the sea driven with the wind and tossed. For let not that man think that he shall receive anything of the Lord" (Jas. i. 6, 7). Thus, without faith in prayer, it is impossible to please God; and, therefore, useless to expect answers to it from God. For, as he who does not believe that God "is," will not seek Him at all; so he that does not believe that God is the rewarder of them that diligently seek Him, will not find Him at all. Unbelieving prayer will always be unprofitable prayer.

We have now before us the three chief principles which regulate the answers to prayer. By them, therefore, let us judge the real character of our own prayers. *First*, Have we prayed humbly? This is a question which we can answer. We know the spirit in which we poured out strong cries and tears unto God for mercy. We remember distinctly how our souls longed, and thirsted, and wrestled for salvation.

We can never forget how a sense of its greatness, and of our own unworthiness, pressed upon our hearts. We saw and felt that there was nothing between us and perishing, but the blood of the Lamb; that we had nothing to say for, but all against ourselves; and that we could do nothing but cry for mercy. Peter, when sinking in the waves—the publican, when smiting on his breast—and the dying thief, when exclaiming, "Lord, remember me!" were at once our examples and our encouragement, during those solemn moments of secret prayer. And though, on looking back to those penitential approaches to God, we feel that they were not so humble as they ought to have been; and remember that, at the time, we felt anxious to sink lower in self-abasement, and ashamed because our spirit was not more broken and contrite; still, when compared with our former state of mind, and when tried by the character of the natural mind, we cannot but think that, whatever else our prayers were then, they were truly humble :—at least, we intended them to be, and tried to make them truly humble. We were not conscious, at the moment, of any pride, or self-dependence. We *meant* nothing of the kind, but were intent upon humbling ourselves before God, and upon repenting in dust and ashes. We were not, indeed, satisfied, at the time, with either our humility or our penitence; but wished both to be deeper. We were not, however, pretending, nor holding back our hearts from shame or sorrow. Accordingly, we feel now, that—whatever else was the defect of our prayers for mercy, and whatever be the result of them—we were not insincere nor heartless in them.

Well, this is the kind of prayer which God has promised to answer. And I thus endeavour to characterise it, and to compare it with prayers which have been answered, that we may see and feel that we have sought the Lord with our whole heart. It is of great importance to be sure of this ; for, whilst we are not sure that we have prayed aright, we cannot believe aright the promises made to the prayerful. Settle it, therefore, in your minds, that as surely as you have mourned, and been in bitterness of soul before God, whilst looking upon the Saviour whom your sins have pierced, so surely has "the spirit of grace and supplication" been poured out upon you from on high. Yes, you have been "taught" to pray, who have thus cried mightily unto God. And as you do not and cannot forget these prayers, neither will God forget or refuse to answer them.

Secondly, Have we had a *holy design* in our prayers? It is of equal importance to be sure of this also. And, as in the former case, we can answer the question. We know whether we are in good earnest to be saved from sin, as well as from hell. We remember distinctly how we felt, and intended, and resolved, in regard to the sins which had dominion over us. There was, indeed, a struggle at the idea of giving them up, and many a fear lest they should regain the mastery. But we did not wish to keep them, nor to come under their bondage again. Our desire was, that God would not only forgive us sins, but also "cleanse us from all iniquity." We knew the fact, and were not dissatisfied with it, that if we regarded sin in our hearts, the Lord would not hear us. In a word, we did not wish to sin because grace abounds, but desired grace for gracious purposes. Thus our prayers were holy in their object, as well as humble in their spirit. Well ; such prayers were never left unanswered. It never was and never will be said in hell, by any one, that he prayed earnestly for holiness, but was denied it. And one reason why this blessing is never denied, is, that whenever it is asked with all the heart, the heart is influenced by the Spirit of God, who never awakens holy desires without intending to gratify them. Settle it, therefore, in your minds, that as surely as you have been led to plead earnestly for a holy salvation, you will be led, by the same Spirit, to rejoice in that salvation eventually. This result cannot fail, because " God cannot lie."

Thirdly, Have we asked in faith, nothing doubting ? Now, here we must at once plead guilty of much unbelief. We have often doubted, and always doubted, more or less, in all our prayers. We can hardly see, in our own case, the possibility of keeping out all doubts from our minds in prayer. Indeed, the thing seems impossible, whatever be the consequence. The consequence is, however, that the doubting man shall receive nothing of the Lord ; and, therefore, undoubting prayer cannot be an impossibility, whatever it may seem at first sight.

This matter must be minutely examined. Now all doubts do not spring from *unbelief;* and many of them are not *wilful.* Accordingly, whilst we are prone to doubt, we take no pleasure in doubting. We should be very glad to be quite free from all doubts and misgivings of heart in prayer. Whatever sin, therefore, may be in them, we fall into it, not willingly, but in order to avoid the far greater sin of *presumption.* So little idea or design have we of offending or dishonouring God by our doubts, that we actually give way to them, lest we should offend Him by hoping too much or too confidently. We think it more becoming and necessary, as sinners, to keep far off from the very appearance of presumption or self-complacency. In a word, we doubt, because we think it would be sinful or rash, in us, to believe that we have obtained the mercy which we have been praying for. Whatever evil, therefore, may be in cherishing the doubts which we indulge, it has certainly been in order to avoid a greater evil, that we have given way to them. This is the real fact of the case ; and, therefore, it does not fall fully under the threatening : "Let not that man think that he shall receive anything of the Lord."

When, however, prayer has been truly humble in its spirit, and holy in its object, it is sinful to entertain any doubt of its success, seeing God has promised, yea, sworn, to answer it. If, indeed, there were no promises, or the promises not "yea and amen" in Christ, doubting might be even a duty or a virtue ; because, in that case, faith would have no clear warrant. But as He who has said, " Ask," has said also, " ye shall receive," it is as much our duty to believe His promise as to obey His precept.

In fact, whatever warrant or reason we have for praying, we have them also for believing that our prayers will be answered. God never said to the seed of Jacob, nor to any one else, " Seek ye my face in vain ;" for " He is not a man that He should lie ; nor the son of man, that He should repent :" " His word standeth fast unto all generations."

" But," some will say, " whatever be argued or proved as to the theory, the fact is, that my prayers for an interest in the salvation of God have not been answered yet. Years have elapsed since I was led to cry mightily unto God for mercy ; but I have not obtained mercy. I do not set this fact against the truth of what I have just read ; but I state it as an exception to the general rule." Now, upon the supposition that you have poured out your heart unto God for saving mercy, I here close with you at once, and ask, Upon what *authority* do you affirm that you have not found mercy of the Lord ? Where has God *said* that He has refused your prayer ? Who told you that you were an *exception* to the general rule ? " I need no one to tell me," you will say ; " my own *feelings* assure me of the fact. Should I not have peace and joy in my heart if my prayers for pardon and acceptance had been answered ? But I am a stranger to peace and joy, and almost to hope too ; and, surely, that is authority and reason enough for saying that my prayers are not answered."

This is, indeed, a strong case, and almost startling to one who has affirmed, and is pledged to confirm the fact, that pardon and acceptance are never denied, when they are earnestly sought for holy purposes. I repeat the fact, however, and proceed to redeem my pledge. Now, you say, that you *feel* that your prayers are not yet answered; accordingly, you *believe* also that they are not. But how would you feel if you believed that your prayers for mercy had been *presented* by the Saviour, and accepted by God? Do you not see, at a glance, that if you believed this to be true, you would *feel* both peace and joy? Well, do you not see, with equal clearness, that whilst you do not believe this, you cannot experience peace or joy? It is impossible to feel the peace of believing, whilst you *disbelieve*. It is unreasonable to expect to feel the answer of prayer, whilst you think that it is unanswered. You cannot *feel* differently from what you *think*. Accordingly, whenever any one has felt his prayers answered, it must have been by believing that Christ had presented them, and that God had thus accepted them, for the sake of Christ.

"But," you say, "I do not know that my prayers have been thus heard at the throne of grace. If I could think that the Saviour had interceded for me, I could then easily believe that I was accepted in the Beloved." Well! Do you know anything to the *contrary?* Can you *prove* that He, who never shut

His ear to the cry of a penitent sinner, has overlooked
you ? Would that be *like* the Saviour's well-known
and long-tried character as the Mediator between
God and man ? Is it not far more in harmony with
all you have read of Him, to believe that, when He
saw you at the foot of the cross crying for mercy, He
took up your cause ? You know that He has taken
up many such, since He took His place as an intercessor before the throne ; and He has not changed
since you began to plead at the footstool.

"True," you say ; "but how can I know that He
has interceded for me ? You say, Believe that your
prayers are accepted through Him ; but where is my
authority or *warrant* for believing this ? Would you
have me to believe it to be true, merely because I
wish it to be true ? I may say here (but in another
spirit), 'What sign showest thou, that we may believe ?'"

Now, you are right in thus requiring a higher
authority than my word, or your own wishes, before
venturing to believe that you have obtained the mercy
of God unto eternal life. Nothing short of a *Divine*
warrant ought to satisfy you ; for nothing less can
sanction a Divine hope. But allow me to ask here,
What do you mean by Divine warrant for believing
that the mercy you implored is granted ? What
would you consider sufficient authority for the belief
of this ? Would the *written word* of God in the
Scriptures satisfy you ? If so, I redeem my pledge at
once : "He that asketh, receiveth ; and he that
seeketh, findeth." Are you disappointed ? Are you

ready to say—" *I have asked, but not received; sought, but not found?*" I am not sure of that. But, were it true that you had not yet found the mercy you have sought, it is equally true that you are warranted, by the express word of God, to believe that you *shall* find it eventually. "Seek, and ye shall find," is the assurance given in Scripture to all the prayerful. And how gloriously Paul amplifies and applies it!—" For whosoever shall call on the name of Lord shall be saved." Here, then, is a Divine warrant for believing that your prayers for salvation *will be* answered; a fact which may well fill your heart with a hope full of immortality, and both increase and confirm your devotional habits.

But even this, pleasing as it is, is not all the truth. If you have prayed like the publican, you are " justified " like the publican. This is the scriptural fact ; and it is by believing it, that peace comes into the mind. In this way only could the publican have known his own justification. No voice from the mercy-seat within the vail answered his prayer for mercy ; no messenger from heaven assured him of pardon ; if, therefore, he went down to his house with a sense of pardon and acceptance, it must have been derived from believing the often revealed fact, that God delighteth in mercy, and is the rewarder of them that diligently seek Him.

This subject cannot, however, be well pursued, until the affinity of fervent prayer and saving faith be clearly understood.

CHAPTER III.

THE AFFINITY OF FERVENT PRAYER AND SAVING FAITH.

HATEVER we may think of prayer, and however doubtful we may feel as to its answer, we are quite sure that faith, when genuine, cannot fail to save the soul. "He that believeth shall never perish." "He that believeth, hath eternal life." Thus real faith places the safety of the soul beyond all risk and doubt. Accordingly, were we as sure that we had *believed* with the heart as that we have *prayed* with the heart—as sure that we are true believers as that we are praying persons, we should then feel that we were both warranted and welcome to consider ourselves the children of God, and to appropriate to ourselves all the great and precious promises. But we are not so sure that we have truly believed, as that we have truly prayed. We have no doubt of the sincerity of our prayers for mercy and grace; but we have many doubts as to the genuineness of our faith. We know when we began to pray in good earnest ; but we cannot tell when we began to believe in Christ with the heart, nor are we sure that our believing is faith. The consequence is, that, whilst thus doubtful of the reality of our faith, we doubt whether our prayers are, or ever will be, answered.

I thus identify myself with you, in your difficulties upon this subject, that I may gain your confidence, and prove to you that I have felt them—felt them so long and deeply—that I have as little inclination to speculate or theorise about faith, as to blaspheme. I have no new system to establish, nor any old ones to explode. What I have studied and prayed to as-certain for myself is—the exact *thing*—the precise *state of mind*, which both God and the Lamb call for, under the *name* of faith or believing ; and with which they have graciously connected the promise of salvation. Now, in examining the word of God on this subject, I find :

First, That the Scriptures do not distinguish between fervent prayer and saving faith; but treat them as the same thing. Both the Old and the New Testament distinguish, and that by the broadest lines of demarca-tion, between faith and *works*—between believing and *doing;* but never between believing and *praying.* Ac-cordingly, there are no instances, in Scripture, of any prayerful person being represented or treated as an *unbeliever*, or without faith. The prayer of the hypo-crite and the wicked is, of course, declared to be "an abomination to the Lord," whilst they continue such ;

but, when the wicked man forsakes his way, and the unrighteous man his thoughts, and turns unto the Lord with supplication, he is recognised and treated as a believer: "God will have mercy upon him, and our God abundantly pardon :" the very promise made to faith. Yea, whenever prayer is humble in its spirit, and holy in its object, it is regarded by God as faith, even if the suppliant be "trembling" at the word of God (Isa. lxvi. 1, 2). "A broken heart," on account of sin, is never represented in Scripture as "an evil heart of unbelief;" nor a "contrite spirit," even if only mourning as without faith : but the promise to mourners in Zion is the very same that Christ made to His real disciples—" They shall be comforted." Even those who are only hungering and thirsting after righteousness (and thus, in their own apprehension, "far from righteousness," and, as some would say, "yet in unbelief"), are not classed with unbelievers, but "blessed" by Him who searcheth the heart, and assured by Him that " they shall be filled."

"This is not the manner of man, O Lord God !" Not the manner of those who make faith to consist in the belief of their own *election :* not the manner of those who make *assurance* the essence of faith : not the manner of those who treat the timid and trembling as unbelievers. It is, however, the manner of Him who is both the object and the judge of faith. He recognises and welcomes the first outgoings and yearnings of the heart towards Him, as manifestations of a believing *disposition*, and as the first fruits of the Spirit.

There is not, then, a moral distinction between prayer and faith : they are not different things in their nature. Why, then, should you distinguish them, seeing the Scriptures do not? If you have prayed with the heart, you have believed with the heart.

Secondly, In farther examining the Scriptures on this subject, I find that they virtually *identify fervent prayer with saving faith.* Not only do they not distinguish between prayer and faith, but they represent them as the same thing in effect, and ascribe to them the same efficacy. Remember the case of the Syrophænician mother : When applying to Christ, on behalf of her daughter, she said nothing about the nature of her faith, nor of its genuineness, but kept on pleading for mercy. Her pleading was her faith. Accordingly, the Saviour called it so : " O woman, great is thy faith; be it unto thee even as thou wilt." It is true that, although she *said* nothing about her faith, she *showed* much faith, by persevering in prayer, notwithstanding many and great discouragements. And have not you done the same? If you have had *no* real faith in Christ—*no* confidence in His blood—*no* high opinion of His gracious heart, would you, *could* you, have continued praying in His name? You may not have been accustomed to hear, and, therefore, not to think, that prayer is the best expression of faith in the Saviour; just as holiness is the best proof of faith in Him. The fact, however, is self-evident the moment it is suggested. You now see, at a glance, that you would not pray at all in the name of Christ, if you had no faith at all in His name; that you would not plead His merits, nor appeal to His blood, if you had no faith in their efficacy; that you would not seek an interest in His salvation, if you did not believe Him to be an all-sufficient Saviour. You do not pray to angels nor to the saints in heaven, as Papists do. Why? Because you have no faith in them. And do you not see, that if you had no faith in Christ, you would not pray to Him either, or in His name? The thing is self-evident.

Consider now the case of the publican. There is nothing said of his faith, and he himself said nothing about it. We see nothing in his case but humble prayer. But we are told that he was "justified;" and, as justification is only by faith alone, it is evident that Christ regarded the publican's prayers as faith. And it is obvious that he never would have prayed as he did for mercy, if he had not believed in the mercifulness of the God of Israel.

Remember, also, the case of the thief on the cross. His application to the Saviour was by prayer: "Lord, remember me when Thou comest into Thy kingdom." Here, indeed, there was much faith expressed and implied; but still it was in the form of prayer, and not more than our prayers express and imply, when we make the blood of Christ all our plea for mercy and grace. And, as the praying malefactor was treated as a believing sinner, we are thus encouraged to pray, and warranted to regard humble prayer as cordial faith.

Remember, also, the case of Paul at Damascus. It was not said, Behold he believeth; but, "Behold he prayeth!" evidently because praying is virtually the same as believing, or the best way of expressing faith. Accordingly, when he became an Apostle, and stood forth as the chief champion of the doctrine of justification by faith alone, he did not distinguish between prayer and faith; but designated as believers, "all that in every place call upon the name of Jesus Christ;" and declared that, "whosoever shall call upon the name of the Lord shall be saved."

Thus it is that the Scriptures teach almost the identity of faith and prayer; and uniformly represent believers as prayerful, and the prayerful as believers. This scriptural fact is of incalculable value, both to those who have been perplexed by the public controversies about faith, and to those who have been perplexed by their own fears and jealousies. Both classes are more numerous than many suppose. But what a pity, and how unnecessary, that the prayerful amongst them should waste their time or their spirits in doubting and discussing the genuineness of their faith! How much better that time would be employed, if devoted to secret prayer. That would bring and keep before the mind, in light and loveliness, the grand *object* of faith—Christ crucified; and when He is before the mind, in the brightness of His glory and the freeness of His grace; in the love of His heart and the omnipotence of His hand; in the all-sufficiency of His sacrifice and the authority of His example, unbelief is overpowered, and fear dispersed, like clouds before the sun.

What, now, do you think of your own case? Your chief difficulty has been, hitherto, to arrive at a satisfactory conclusion as to the reality of your faith in Christ. Sometimes you have suspected that it was a mere *historical* faith. But does historical faith *pray* fervently? At other times you have thought it no better than the faith of *devils*. But devils do not *pray* whatever they may believe. You have also thought it *dead* faith. But does dead faith *pray* earnestly? You have often thought it the mere faith of education or custom—that vague and vapid kind of believing which *any one* can practise, and which every one professes. But does this current faith lead into the *closet* with strong cries and tears for mercy? I would not, for worlds, flatter you; but I must say, that if you are in the habit of praying with the heart in secret, and in the name of Christ, and for a holy salvation, your faith is "the faith of God's elect."

"But," some one may say, "I find it quite as difficult to know if I pray aright as if I believe aright. I am as much ashamed of my prayers as of my faith. Sometimes I cannot pray at all; at other times my prayers are hurried and heartless; and at all times they are so imperfect that I can hardly see how God can answer them." This is a very common complaint and a familiar acknowledgment. What, however, do you really mean to confess by this form of words? Do you mean to say that you only *pretend* when you pray for mercy? That you are *insincere* when you ask for salvation? That you feel no need of them, nor care whether you obtain them or not? Do you mean that in using the name of Christ, and referring to His blood, you think nothing about them, or see no value in them? If, indeed, such be the character of your prayers, you may well say that you cannot see how God can answer them. He never did, and never will, answer hypocritical prayers.

But this is not what you mean. Well, do you mean to say that you were never in *earnest* about the salvation of your soul?—never *felt* what you said when confessing your sins and seeking an interest in the Saviour?—never wept, nor *wished* to weep tears of penitence before God? In a word, do you mean to say that you never felt anything of the spirit of the publican when he smote upon his breast, and cried, "God be merciful to me a sinner?" If so, why do you call your heartless words prayers? But this is not what you mean. You are shocked at such an idea, and wonder how I could suspect you of such impiety. The fact is, I have no suspicion of the kind, but have had recourse to these questions, just that you may discover your own *sincerity* amidst all the imperfections of your prayers. What you mean chiefly is, that though at times you have felt a humble and broken spirit, and could weep before God, and pour out all your heart, yet more frequently you have been cold and formal. You mean, too, that you are sadly harassed by vain and wandering thoughts, even when you are upon your knees before God ; and that often when you even wish to enjoy communion with Him, your heart will neither fix nor feel as you desire. But all this is your grief and shame. You are not *reconciled* to such praying. You do not like, you dislike, the bare idea of going on in this way. Nothing would please you more than getting over these hinderances. You are never so happy as when you unburden and unbosom all your soul before God, and throw all your heart into every word you utter. You can never *forget* the hallowed moments of retirement when you first caught the spirit of prayer, and felt what it is to commune with God at the mercy-seat. You understand at once what MELANCTHON meant, when he said of LUTHER, "I have overheard him in secret prayer ; and he spoke as if God had been in the closet with him." You can well believe this of Luther ; for you have at times felt as if God was in your closet. Accordingly, what you want is, to get back to this devotional spirit and to continue in it. No wonder ! There is, however, quite as much that is pleasing to God in the broken sighs and unutterable groanings of a contrite spirit, as in the ardours of sensible communion. A heart shrinking from and resisting vain thoughts, and struggling to throw off the world and flesh is, perhaps, as fully approved by Him who searcheth the heart, as when—

> " On eagle pinions borne,
> It climbs the mount of God."

What do you think, now, of the sentiment, that whosoever hath really prayed with the heart for a holy salvation hath actually believed with the heart? You are, perhaps, equally afraid to admit or deny it. It is, perhaps, somewhat *new* to you; and if it be altogether new to you, you ought to suspend your judgment upon it, until you have examined it more fully. You cannot be too jealous of *novelties* in religion. It does not, however, follow because a truth is new to you, that it is new in itself. The *spirituality* of the Divine law is as old as the law itself; but it was treated as a novelty by the Jews, when Christ explained and enforced it upon the mount, because they had made void the law by the traditions of men. In this case it was the gloss of the elders that was the real novelty, and the doctrine of Christ that was the old truth. In like manner Popery, although ancient in reference to time, is in reference to Scripture a real novelty; and the Protestant creed, the old faith of the Christian Church. It is not, therefore, the length of time during which mystical views of faith have been current that stamps them correct. Their long currency is itself a reason for suspecting their correctness, especially when the effect of them upon the truly serious and prayerful is discouraging. For that cannot be a right view of faith, however old it may be, which makes salvation appear as difficult by the Gospel as it is by the law, or as far off by faith as it is by works. There must be something awfully defective in every definition of faith which discourages or perplexes a soul intent upon obtaining an interest in Christ and conformity to His image. The whole Gospel is intended and calculated to meet the wishes of every such soul; and therefore if our views of faith only tantalise these wishes, or make that Gospel to appear other than "good news" to us, those views must be erroneous in something; and to contend for them is to contend against the Gospel itself.

This, I am fully aware, is not intended by those who teach, nor by those who hold mystical views of faith. Nothing, I am persuaded, is farther from their hearts, than to defeat or encumber the Gospel. Their real design is to exalt and maintain that Gospel above the unholy level of slight and superficial views, and to secure a faith "full of good fruits." But still if this system really prevent faith, and make the Gospel appear as unmanageable as the law, no excellence of motive must be allowed to shield it from solemn reprehension. The express language of the Scriptures is, that faith is the hearty belief of the truth concerning the person and work of Christ; and that the best expression of believing with the heart, is praying with the heart. This definition of faith is so simple that any one can understand it at once; and if it appear at all new to you, the novelty is not in itself, but in your notice of the fact; for the fact itself is as old as the Bible. In like manner if, in reference to some old theological definitions of faith, it seems new, it merely *sounds* new; for in

Scripture the prayerful are always treated as true believers.

But it will be said, that the old definitions of faith are chiefly derived from the old divines; and that such remarks implicate them. Did not Owen and Baxter, Hervey and Henry, Watts and Doddridge, Boston and the *old* Erskines, understand faith?

Understand faith! Yes, and possessed, too, infinitely more of it than any writer who has arraigned them. They were "full of faith;" and it was their fulness which gave rise to that cast of mystery and indefiniteness which characterises some of their explanations of faith. They were, in fact, so full of the *thing*, that they could not find a simple *name* for it. Words were the least part of their explanations of faith; their *spirit* was the living illustration of its meaning. There was no mist around the subject, whilst these thoughtful and devotional men were pouring all their soul into their sermons. Their hearers could then see that, however faith was defined, the real essence of it was a right state of mind towards the Saviour, and that prayer was the best expression of it. It is, therefore, only when men of "*little faith*" employ the complex names by which the old divines designated and described faith, that confusion is created. It is their words, when in the lips of men without their spirit, which "darken knowledge," and occasion perplexity. Accordingly, all the truly *devotional* men, who have clear views of faith, find no difficulty (but unspeakable delight) in the deep thoughts and holy unction of the old divines. Their adoring and realising views of the Lamb slain, arrange themselves gloriously around definite expressions. All their vague modes of expression on the subject of faith are forgotten in the presence of their vast and radiant ideas of the great salvation. "The savour of the knowledge of Christ" is always full and fresh in their pages. In a word, they perplex none but those who have never studied the subject, and offend none but the fastidious, and those who prefer names to things.

It must be allowed, and may be regretted, that the old divines do not always express themselves clearly upon the subject of faith. As the *name* of what God and the Lamb call for, faith is often equivocal in their pages ; but the *thing*—the state of mind required by the Gospel, beams, yea blazes throughout their writings. Christ is "all in all" in their own religion, and their sole aim is to make Him so in the religion of others. Accordingly, no man seriously inquiring the way of salvation, ever rose from their works, under an impression that they were leading him *away* from the cross of Christ, to his own righteousness. Many have felt that some of the old writers lead inquirers in rather a *round-about* way to the cross ; but they have felt at the same time, even when that route was most circuitous, that it was only to make their arrival more certain. The slowness is always for the sake of *sureness*, and never for self-righteous purposes.

No one owes these acknowledgements to the old

divines more than I do, and no one makes them with greater sincerity. I prefer, infinitely, their *state of mind* towards the Saviour, to all the theories of faith extant. It was a living lecture on the whole subject, and the chief reason of its being misunderstood by some, and misrepresented by others, is that they have not *spirituality* enough to enter into the spirit of these " men of God." Their words, in unbaptized, and even in half-baptized lips, must always lose more than half their meaning, and convey to others still less of it. They, in fact, defined faith as a fond mother would define her *love* to her first-born ; not logically nor literally, but with an abundance of words, corresponding to the abundance of their feelings. " Out of the abundance of the heart, the mouth speaketh," is the real explanation of their system.

But whilst I thus heartily, though imperfectly, attempt to do justice to the memory and writings of the old divines, I do not forget that their works are not the word of God. They themselves never intended that their definitions of faith should, in anywise, defeat or encumber the Gospel. The most voluminous amongst the Puritans would have burned or re-written their folios, if they had suspected them of any such tendency. They had, however, no such tendency at the time : they were written agreeably to the modes of speaking in use then. And, as our modes of expression are fewer and more definite, what is wanted is, not an exposure of their defects, but a full return to the language of Scripture.

The word of God is able to make us wise unto salvation, if all the other books in the world were annihilated; and it ought to be consulted and submitted to, without any reference to them as authorities. If, therefore, you have derived from any human writings, or from any human source, such an idea of faith as makes *believing aright* appear to you as difficult as *obeying perfectly*, you cannot abandon it too soon, whoever be the author of it. Whoever he was, he did not intend that his definition of faith should make faith seem an impossibility in your case. He drew it out, in the first instance, for *himself;* and, therefore, you may be sure that it did not appear to him what it seems to you. He saw it in a light that left his own way and welcome to the cross quite open; and, under this impression, he gave it to the public, in hope that the definition would open their way. But if it *shut* you out, then all that you know of its author (and the more that is good the better for my argument), warrants and binds you to give up his definitions, and to throw yourself at once upon the words which the Holy Ghost teacheth.

But this digression is already too long. Let us return to the direct subject of the essay—the *oneness* of faith and prayer. Now you feel the necessity of faith. You are anxious to possess it. You have often tried to exercise faith in the Saviour. You have occasionally felt as if the emotions and desires of your hearts towards Him were ripening into real faith. But still you are not satisfied. You are far from sure whether you have, indeed, believed with the heart. If, however, you are sure that you have prayed with the heart, there is no occasion for all this uncertainty on the question of faith. For it is self-evident that, if you had *no* faith in Christ, you would not offer up all your prayers in the name of Christ, nor make His merits your only plea at the mercy-seat.

It is, indeed, true that thousands unite, every Sabbath, in prayers which make the merits of Christ the sole plea; and yet evince no faith. But theirs is not a parallel case to yours. Mercy is the inmost desire of your heart, and the blood of Christ your only ground of hope. You can no longer be satisfied with repeating *words*, however good. You must now express *desires;* and sometimes they are so many and strong, that you cannot find words to express them. And such is your state of mind, in reference to your own salvation, that neither the number nor the nature of your prayers satisfy you. It is just what you see in Christ, and not what you see in them, that keeps you praying. You feel that, but for what He *is* and has *done*, you must soon despair and perish. It is not your prayers, but His merits, which give you any hope.

Now, such being the facts of your case, it is really unwise, if not criminal, to question the reality of your faith. Its weakness is very obvious; but its *sincerity* is self-evident. No unbeliever could pray in this spirit. There is no instance in Scripture of any unbeliever crying mightily unto God for mercy, through the blood of the Lamb. It is, indeed, difficult to say how far wicked men may go at times, in praying for mercy in the name of Christ. You have, no doubt, known men who could pray with wonderful fervour, and with every appearance of sincerity, and who have been found out afterwards to have been living in gross sin at the very time. Neither public nor social prayer, however remarkable, is, therefore, any sure test of faith or sincerity. Secret prayer is the test. The men who can pray and drink, pray and lie, pray and defraud, pray and be profligate—do not, dare not pray in their closets. Secret sin cannot be combined with secret prayer. The yet unmasked sensualist may, at times, be forced by fear to fall down alone before God, and break the silence of the night by the groans of remorse; but if he continue to sin, he will soon discontinue secret prayer. His closet will be more intolerable to him than even the sanctuary, whilst he persists in sinning against light and conviction.

These solemn facts ought never to be forgotten; but, except as tests of character, and warnings of danger, what have they to do with your case? You want to be saved from sin, as well as from the curse. You are willing and solicitous to be holy, as well as safe. It is not because some vice still enslaves you, that you are afraid lest your prayers should not be answered, or that your faith may prove vain. Your fear arises chiefly from what you have been as a sinner, and from what you are as a penitent. The past alarms you by its guilt, and the present by its imperfections. It is not, however, *actual* nor *habitual* sinning now, that clouds your mind with doubts and fears. Your present difficulty (and it is a pressing one), is to see how prayers, so imperfect as yours, can be answered or accepted by God, especially as you are not sure that you pray in faith. Here is your chief discouragement : not only all the "plagues" of your heart seem to forbid hope, but you suspect that it is still "an evil heart of unbelief;" and knowing that without faith it is impossible to please God, you are thus afraid at times to hope or pray. And yet you cannot give up either altogether. Well, you have no occasion to give up hoping or praying ; for praying with the heart is believing with the heart.

This is, I am aware, merely bringing the matter to the same point again, without any additional proof of the truth of that point. More proof is, however, at hand. Now, nothing can be conceived as more opposite or unlike to *unbelief* than humble prayer, in the name of Christ, for a holy salvation. Whatever difficulty you may find, therefore, in calling such prayer faith, it is certainly impossible to call it unbelief, without violating all propriety. UNBELIEF, even when in its softest form, is careless about salvation ; indifferent to the Saviour ; averse to prayer; heedless of holiness ; and not afraid of the wrath to come. Unbelief is not ashamed of itself, nor much shocked at sin, except when sin is very gross indeed. Unbelief has no ardent longings after union with

Christ, or communion with God. Unbelief does not try to get hold of the promises, nor pray for their fulfilment. Unbelief does not weep at the foot of the cross, nor rejoice to go to the mercy-seat.

This is UNBELIEF! But this is not the state of your mind towards the salvation or the service of God and the Lamb. Almost the very *reverse* of this is the real state of your feelings and desires. Thank God, therefore, and take courage !

CHAPTER IV.

WHOEVER has a praying spirit, has both the work and witness of the Holy Spirit begun within him. All real suppliants are really partakers of the Spirit of grace and supplication. Were this well understood, and habitually remembered by the prayerful, it would both confirm their love to prayer, and settle that absorbing question—Am I born again of the Spirit? This solemn question has often made you solemn. It has occasionally agitated your whole soul. No wonder: for "if any man," however moral or amiable, "have not the spirit of Christ, He is none of His." "Except a man be born of the Spirit, he cannot enter into the kingdom of God." Ever since you read those solemn oracles, so as to mark and inwardly digest them, you have felt that saving piety is more than a mere good character, and that personal religion is more than the discharge of religious duties. These "true sayings of God" have turned your attention in upon the state of your heart, as well as out upon the state of your morals. You feel now that you must "be born again," if you would enter the kingdom of God. Your convictions on this point are gone so far beyond those of Nicodemus, that it is needless to say unto you, "Marvel not that ye must be born again." You have ceased to "marvel" at the necessity of a change of heart, ever since you discovered the plagues of your own heart. Any marvelling you ever felt has given place to praying for a new heart and a right spirit. To be the subject of the work and witness of the Holy Spirit is now your chief concern, and your daily prayer. And your chief fear is, lest that Spirit, whom you have grieved so often, and neglected so long, should refuse to take away the heart of stone, or to give you a heart of flesh. You even feel, at times, as if He had refused to work upon your soul, and ceased to strive with you. And even when these strivings are renewed, you are afraid that they do not amount to the *saving* operations of the Holy Spirit, because they do not produce such a change of heart as you desire to experience. And even when you are almost convinced that what you have experienced is the beginning of His work on your heart, how often are all your fond hopes overthrown again by the questions—"But where is the witness of the Spirit with my spirit? If I were, indeed, born of the Spirit, would He not witness within me, that I am a child of God?"

Such are some of your ponderings and perplexities

upon this solemn subject. Sometimes you think that the Holy Spirit has given you up entirely; at other times, that what you feel is only His common, not His special, influence ; and even when it is best with you, you are, as you imagine, such a stranger to the witness of the Spirit, that you can take but little comfort from what you feel of His work. Much of this fear is, however, really unnecessary ; for it chiefly arises from misapprehending the work and witness of the Holy Spirit. A spirit of prayer is proof of the possession of something of both, in the case of all who are looking to Christ, and trying to be holy. Prayer, even if secret, proves nothing of the work or witness of the Spirit, in the case of those who are going on in open or secret sin. The sensual have not the Spirit. But where prayer is loved, and not belied by sensuality or dishonesty, it is itself the first fruit of the Spirit, and positive evidence of His saving operations being begun in the heart.

Did this never occur to your mind in the course of all your ponderings on the subject ? Who inclined your heart to pray ? Who overcame the aversion and reluctance you once felt to pouring out your heart unto God in secret ? " Who opened thine eyes " to see your need of an interest in Christ so clearly, that you can no longer refrain from praying to " be found in Him ? " Who brought you to feel that there is nothing between you and hell but the blood of Christ ? Who awakened your present convictions and desires ? Here is a change, and a change for the better, in the state of your mind : who produced it ? If you are afraid to ascribe it to the Spirit of God, to what can you trace it ? Satan would not teach you such lessons ; and, certainly, the example of the world has not led you into your closet to cry for mercy and grace. Your trials in life may have had much to do with that change ; but the fact, instead of disproving it to be a Divine change, makes it more than probable that it is so ; for nothing is more common, in the work of the Spirit, than to sanctify the trials of life to the good of the soul. In every view of the case, therefore, it is your duty to regard the change, from a prayerless to a prayerful spirit, as the effect of Divine influence and operation. There is no other way of accounting for it satisfactorily or rationally. It is a " good gift " so far ; and, therefore, it must have come " down from the Father of lights." You will be convinced of this, by observing how your views and feelings in prayer correspond with the scriptural accounts of the work of the Spirit. Paul says, " The Spirit maketh inter- cession for us with groanings which cannot be uttered." Thus, he ascribes to the Holy Spirit's special interces- sion a kind of prayer which we hardly regard as prayer at all. We are apt to think that we do not pray " in the Spirit," unless we enjoy great enlargement of heart, and freedom of utterance. Accordingly, the devotional hours, which we recollect with most pleasure, and which we can never forget, are those which were marked with a holy calm—a sweet melan- choly, and a free flow of tears, and tenderness, and suitable words. Then we felt that the Spirit was, indeed, helping our infirmities ! And could we always, or even often, pray in that manner, we should almost feel warranted to believe that we had the seal of the Spirit upon our souls. But as it is not often that we enjoy such enlargement of heart, we hardly know, at times, what to think of our experience.

Now, it is not to divert your attention or your love from this kind of prayer, that I remind you of another kind, which, if less pleasing to you, is, perhaps, more pleasing to God, and certainly more decisive of the help and presence of the Spirit. " Groanings which cannot be uttered," prove, far more than any flow of words or feelings, that the heart is right with God, and that the Holy Spirit is working mightily in it. We may look back with shame upon those approaches to the mercy-seat, during which we could hardly utter a single word, but merely groaned in spirit : but the Intercessor before the throne was not ashamed to present those desires to the Father, nor to say of them, " A broken and a contrite heart, O God, thou wilt not despise." He saw in those unutterable groans and deep sighs, not the accidental workings of our own nature, but the workings of "a Divine nature," struggling against the body of sin and death—the strivings of the Spirit against the flesh. Yes, when you thought that you were not praying at all, while thus groaning under the burden of your sin and unworthiness, you were praying best. And were the Saviour to say to you, as to Nathanael, " When thou wast under the fig-tree, I saw thee," he would undoubtedly refer chiefly to the times when you were so troubled in spirit that you could not speak.   The prayers we have most cause to be ashamed of are those which we can go through without effort or feeling.   We are not praying at all whilst merely repeating words.   Nothing is prayer but the desires of the heart; and they are never so fully or directly from the Spirit of God, as when they are unutterable by words.   Indeed, this is a state of mind quite *unnatural* to man.   There is nothing in us, nor in human means, to produce it.   It gets no help from any power or affection of our nature.   Imagination will help the prayer of joy, and the prayer of faith, and the prayer of gratitude : but not the humble prayer of penitence.   It is from the " intercession " of the Spirit.

Now you know, experimentally, something of this kind of prayer.   There are times when a sense of your own unworthiness comes over your soul like a heavy and suffocating cloud.   You can hardly breathe under it.   You feel as if your heart would break, it is so full and so heavy.   It is only now and then that you are able to groan out the cry of Job, " Behold, I am vile."   The prayer of the publican is not humble enough for your sinking spirit : you would go deeper in self-abasement if you knew how.   You abhor yourself, and lay your face in the dust before God.   You are terrified at despair, yet afraid to hope.   You can hardly see how God *can* pity you.   It seems to you almost presumption to pray for mercy ; and when you do, it is by a groan or a sigh. These are solemn moments! The silence is so deep, and we are so alone with God, that we are afraid to speak. God, in His majesty, is before us; eternity, in its solemnity, is before us; and were it not that we still see something of the CROSS amidst the overwhelming scene, we feel that life or reason must fail under it. You remember these moments; but you remember also that you did not think then that you were praying, far less that you were praying in the Spirit. You left your closet on those nights, ashamed and confounded, that you could not pray. You felt yourself as far off from the mercy of God as you felt near to the majesty of God. One wish that often passed through your heart was, that the Holy Spirit would help your infirmities, and enable you to pray. You had no idea that he was working in you mightily at the moment, and never more gracious to you. But, verily, God was with you then, as with Jacob on Bethel, although you "knew it not" at the time.

Does this view of the matter surprise you at all? It ought not in the least: for, if you look back to those seasons of unutterable groanings, you will soon recollect that you never were more humble before God; never more self-condemned, or self-emptied, than when your spirit was so pained within you that you could not speak. It was then, especially, that you saw and felt that God would be *just* even if He condemned you; that you could say nothing *against* His law or His Gospel, however their penal sanctions might sink you ; that you had deserved all the curse, and none of the blessing, of God. You felt through all your soul also, that you were entirely, and must be eternally, at the disposal of the Divine *will;* and that there was, indeed, nothing between you and perishing but the blood of Christ. You did not see, at the time, how the atonement met all the difficulties in your case; but you saw nothing else that met any of them. Everything else, as a ground of hope, appeared to you a mere refuge of lies. The Lamb slain had all your attention ; and any hope you ventured to cherish sprung from His cross and character. You had not, indeed, much hope in Him, and still less confidence, but you had none in anything else. Now, what was all this but the Spirit fulfilling in you the promise of Christ concerning His work : " He shall convince of sin, and of righteousness, and of judgment ?" The grand end of the Spirit's office is "to glorify" the Saviour ; and the Saviour is never more glorified than when the soul is brought to look away, and flee away, from every thing to Him. This is the Spirit's *foundation-work* in the soul, when He is about to dwell in the heart.

Remember also the influence which those solemn seasons had upon your character and habits. How thoughtful, watchful, and steady you became, under the solemn consciousness that your eternal all was in jeopardy ! How it tamed your levity, and broke down your pride, to find that you could not pray, nor, of yourself, think a good thought ! You were never so little, nor so low in your own esteem, as when you rose from your knees, unable to pray but in broken sighs and burning tears. Your character was never better than whilst you had to leave your closet, day after day, saying to yourself—" Well, it must all rest on the will of God ; for I can do nothing but groan for mercy. If prayer could save me, I cannot pray. ' Lord, I am oppressed, undertake for me.' " You did not think lightly of sin then, nor expose yourself to temptation. You took no liberties with the Sabbath then, and had no relish for worldly pleasures. The Bible was not the least read book on your table then, nor its pages hastily read. A prayer-meeting was not a tame nor tedious service then, but a sweet help under your own difficulties in praying. Your spirit and deportment improved, too, under your humbling sense of your own weakness and unworthiness. You were meeker, gentler, and less easily offended than formerly. You were afraid of anger, and of peevishness, and of all jangling, lest they should make all that was bad in the closet worse. You had neither time nor inclination to fret yourself about the trifles which vex those who care little about their souls. In a word, many of the best parts of your character, and of your habits in life, were actually formed whilst you were hanging between hope and despair, and groaning in spirit before the Lord.

I do not mean, of course, that your happier moments in prayer were less holy in their direct influence. Sweet communion with God in prayer is sure to have a sweet influence upon our temper and habits, because we have then something worth taking care of, and too valuable to be sacrificed for the sake of trifles. A man whose closet is really a Bethel, and whose heart is happy in the consciousness of the Divine presence, will do much and suffer much, rather than open the door to either ill-humour or useless pursuits. He knows by experience how easily the veil is drawn upon the mercy-seat, and how difficult it is to undraw it again; and therefore watches both his temper and his habits, that they may not get between him and the "face of the throne." Indeed, he can neither indulge ill habits nor ill humours, whilst he maintains "fellowship with the Father and with the Son." It is, therefore, no wonder that we refer to the help of the Holy Spirit those prayers chiefly which make us happiest, seeing they also make us holiest. Much, however, of their holy influence arises from the prior influence of "the groanings which cannot be uttered." They laid, or dug, the foundations of our religious character; and, but for these straits in prayer, we should either have not prized enlargement, or not improved it fully.

I thus remind you of the humbling and sanctifying influence of our *speechless* prayers (which we did not think prayers at the time), that you may see clearly their Divine origin. They are the intercession of the Spirit, excited and sustained by Him as the teacher and helper of the Church.

CHAPTER V.

ERE we fully aware of the full meaning of our words, when we say that God is the Hearer of prayer, Christ the Intercessor for prayer, and the Holy Spirit the Helper in prayer, we could not pray without deep solemnity and real pleasure. The amazing fact that the sacred Trinity unite in equal attention to prayer, could not fail, if duly weighed and vividly realised, to awe and animate our souls, whenever we knelt at the mercy-seat. But, alas! though in one sense quite familiar with this sweet and sublime fact, it is not often that we pray under its sweet and solemn influence. Accordingly, it is almost a *new* fact to us, both when we see it vividly presented by others, and when we ourselves enter into the spirit of it. Then, like Job, we resolve our past impressions of God into " the hearing of the ear," and exclaim : " But now —mine eye seeth Thee."

It is, indeed, humiliating to acknowledge that our

realising views of Father, Son, and Spirit, being equally
interested in prayer, should be so few and far between.
It is, however, only too true ; and it is necessary to
acknowledge it to ourselves fully, that we may set upon
ascertaining its causes and cure. Many of its causes
are, indeed, easily ascertained. We sometimes hurry
into the presence of God, and even hurry over the duty
of prayer. Instead of pausing to compose our spirits,
or to collect our scattered thoughts by reading a portion of the Scriptures, we often enter at once upon the
duty. In like manner, we do not in general *expect* to
enjoy communion with God, nor to find much pleasure
in our closets. We are even in danger of taking for
granted, that intimate communion with God is not
often to be obtained. We have heard it spoken of as
a special privilege ; and thus we imagine that it must,
of course, be a rare thing. And when these misappre-
hensions and hurries are combined with any degree of
a bad conscience towards God or man, it is no wonder
that our realising views of the Divine presence are
both few and feeble. For how could they be other-
wise, whilst we expect little, and prepare less ? Oh, it
was not thus, it could not be thus, that the disciples
entered their closets to pray after the day of Pentecost!
When they *knew* fully that the Spirit would help their
infirmities, and that their ascended Lord would intercede for them, and that their heavenly Father would
hear and answer prayer, they could not have knelt
without awe, nor pleaded without hope. It was impossible, whilst these glorious facts were before them,

in all their *freshness*, that they could be formal or heartless in devotion; for, next to the open vision of the throne of grace in heaven, is the vivid belief of the truth concerning that throne;—it is, indeed, " the evidence of things not seen, and the substance of things hoped for."

If you have not fully realised this, or if you find it difficult to do so, there is, perhaps, nothing human could help you so much as a calm consideration of the case of the disciples, when they understood clearly the arrangements of heaven for hearing prayer. The disciples, although gradually introduced to an acquaintance with the nature of prayer, did not, like us, grow up familiar, from their youth, with all the facts of the subject. Some of the chief facts flashed out upon them suddenly and unexpectedly. They never dreamt of such a thing as the intercession of Christ, or the help of the Spirit in prayer, until the facts were revealed to them on the day of Pentecost. All this, as we know it, was entirely *new* to them. They were not, indeed, utter strangers, before, to the office of the Father, Son, and Spirit, in relation to prayer. They were even well acquainted with the paternal character of God, and had heard much of the efficacy of the " Name" of Christ in connection with prayer. In like manner, they were not entirely ignorant of the work of the Holy Spirit; but knew as much of the whole subject as made them very prayerful. Their knowledge, however, came far short of the amazing and magnificent fact,—that the enthroned Saviour ever liveth to intercede for them ; and the eternal Spirit, to help their infirmities in prayer ! This was almost completely new to them, and must have given almost a new aspect to prayer itself. Whatever they expected from the promises that Christ would remember them, and that the Spirit would help them, was far exceeded, and almost eclipsed, by the glory of that remembrance, and the grace of that help. They felt, if not said, when the promise was fulfilled, " the half was not told us!"

You perceive that this is a fair statement of their case, so far. Imagine, then, with what solemnity and delight the disciples retired, for the first time, to pray, with these facts, in all the freshness of their glory, vividly before them. If their closets had been the gate of heaven before, how much more widely that gate was opened then ! Then they could see Jesus before the throne, presenting their prayers, embalmed with the incense of His actual intercession. Then they could calculate upon help from the Holy Spirit, not only in their public work, but also in their private warfare against sin and Satan. How they must have prayed the *first* night that all this was revealed to them ! With what looks they must have met, with what emphasis said to each other, when they knew it, Jesus ever liveth to intercede for us ! The Holy Spirit helpeth us to pray, as well as to preach!

I thus try to depict the whole scene, that you may easily realise it, and feel how impossible it is to pray coldly, whilst the intercession of Christ and the help of the Spirit are clearly before the mind. You see, you feel, that the disciples never could have prayed before as they did that night. You feel that, had you been one of them, you must, like them, have been amazed and melted by the discovery of these facts. Well, the facts themselves are the same. Their value does not depend upon a *sudden* discovery of them. You have come to the knowledge of them gradually ; but you do know them, and can set yourself to realise them. You have, whilst reading these imperfect hints, shaken off something of your cold familiarity with them, and felt that it is possible to shake off more of it. You have caught a glimpse of the right way of looking at the office of the Son and Spirit, in the case of prayer. You are resolved to recollect this hint to-night, when you retire to kneel at the mercy-seat.

It may be, however, that the very clearness with which you now see the amazing fact, that the Holy Spirit does *help* in prayer, makes you doubt whether you have ever experienced His help in prayer. You may feel afraid to refer your own earnest supplications to a source so high. It seems too good news to be true, that the Eternal Spirit should have inclined our hearts to pray, and enabled us to pray according to the will of God ! It is really more difficult to admit this to be true in our own case, than it was for " holy men of old" to believe their own inspiration. In speaking as the Spirit moved them, the movements of the Spirit were so sensible and extraordinary, that the prophets could not doubt the reality of their inspiration. But, in our case, the drawing and opening of the heart to pray, have been so gradual, and are so partial, that it seems presumption to ascribe such a slender effect to such a majestic cause. We know, and can never forget, how imperfect and impure our best prayers have been. As acts of our own understanding and conscience, we are ashamed of them; how then can we connect them with the operations of the Spirit of God? We feel our prayers to be unworthy of the natural powers of our own spirit; how much more of the Divine power of the Holy Spirit!

The man who has never felt this deeply, has never thought deeply upon the subject. Oh! it is no easy matter to say, " with the understanding," the Eternal Spirit has helped *my* infirmities in prayer! It is easy to talk and argue about the influences, operations, and outpourings of the Spirit; but to say, as in the presence of God, I have *felt* them, and know experimentally that the Holy Spirit has welcomed and helped me to pray,—he must think twice before he speak once, who speaks thus. You feel this; and are, perhaps, becoming more afraid than ever to admit the amazing fact in your own case. You have been pleased and profited by secret devotion, and have thought at the time that surely the Spirit was helping your infirmities; but, now that the solemn grandeur of that help is breaking out upon you, you dare hardly believe that ever *you* have been really a partaker of it! Perhaps, some doubts of its reality, in any case, are forcing themselves upon your mind, and compelling you to ask—Does the Holy Spirit help at all now in prayer?

Bringing the matter to this point may, indeed, agitate and unhinge you for a moment; but it will do you no real harm. It will do you real good, by drawing you off from taking things for granted, to the better plan of proving all things. I want to give truth the *force* of truth upon your mind, that you " may know what you say, and whereof you affirm," whenever you speak of the office or operations of the Holy Spirit. For if you are really staggered by these views of the matter, it is certain that you have never examined the matter fully. If you think it at all doubtful, whether the Spirit still helps the infirmities of the prayerful, you have never looked steadfastly upon the facts of the case. For what are the facts in regard to the continued help of the Spirit? Why, one of them is, that the denial of it involves the virtual overthrow of the whole Gospel. The work of the Spirit, and the truth of the Word, stand or fall together. The men who have denied or derided the doctrine of the Spirit's influences, might just as well have denied that God *hears* prayer, or that Christ *intercedes* for the prayerful. For there is nothing implied in all the work of the Holy Spirit that is less credible, or less rational, or less likely, than what is implied in the work of the Father and the Son. If the Father can hear, the Spirit can help; if the Son can intercede, the Spirit can assist. Why, then, if I am not visionary when I say, " God will hear me," should I be called so, or think myself so, when I say, " the Spirit will help me?" Even natural religion admits that the Father of our spirits has access to our spirits, and may influence them. Some deists have even prayed to God for Divine direction. Unless, therefore, I were to become an atheist, or to deny that God can hear prayer, I cannot be visionary whilst believing that He who condescends to hear it will condescend to help it. Thus triumphantly, you see, the help of the Spirit may be demonstrated. It is, indeed, wonderful that the Eternal Spirit should act upon our hearts, and draw out their desires after salvation and holiness ; but not at all more wonderful than that the Father should listen to the expression of these desires, or that there is such a " great salvation " to pray for. It is just because the work of Christ is so valuable and glorious, that the work of the Spirit is so sure and constant. Thus there is no more reason to doubt whether the Spirit continues to help on earth, than whether the Father continues to hear, or the Son to intercede in heaven.

But if these hints establish your faith in the fact that the Spirit does help the prayerful, they increase, perhaps, your fears in your own case. Now that you see that the help is as rational as it is necessary, you hesitate whether to ascribe to the work of the Holy Spirit the workings of your own spirit in prayer. For although you have at times felt deeply, and wept sincerely, and cried fervently, and resolved solemnly before the throne of grace, you now suspect that even all this hardly comes up to what is included in *Divine help*. You imagine, that if a "spirit of grace and supplication" had really been poured out upon you, you would have felt far more than all this. You can scarcely conceive how a day of such "small things" can be the fruit of so great a Spirit! This is a trying dilemma. Your mind is alive to the truth and glory of help from on high; but both the truth and glory of it make you afraid that you are not a partaker of it. You are unwilling to admit that you are an utter stranger to the influences of the Holy Spirit; and yet you are unable to say, with certainty, that you are a subject of them. You wish to be so—have sought to be so—and have occasionally hoped that you were so! but some of these hints have thrown you out of your usual track of thinking, and startled you so that you cannot yet recover yourself. It is, however, a good sign to be concerned about the work of the Spirit, and afraid of mistaking it; "for they who are after the Spirit, mind the things of the Spirit;" whereas they who are after the flesh, mind only the things of the flesh. Upon this scriptural fact I have often been glad to take my stand, when, like you, I have felt utterly unable or afraid to answer the solemn question, "Have ye received the Holy Spirit?" I durst not say yes; and to say no, was intolerable. I could only say, "Thou who knowest all things, knowest that I mind the things of the Spirit; that I am concerned and intent upon understanding them, and praying to be a partaker of them." Now, you can truly say this; and, therefore, do—cling to this until you are enabled to say more.

Your great difficulty, now that you see the help of the Holy Spirit to be a reality, is, that nothing which you have experienced seems to come up to it. The Spirit is an Almighty Agent; and you cannot think that His work in the heart could be so weak as it is in your heart. I recollect being sorely pressed by this difficulty, whilst walking in the fields one day alone. It was in the summer, when the insects were sporting in the sun. It occurred to me, whilst gazing upon them, that each of these tiny insects was as much the work of Omnipotence as the mightiest angel; that its almost inaudible hum could only have been called forth by the same power which inspires the hymn of the archangel. I then saw in a moment that "small things," in the beginning of a work of grace, may be as really the work of the Spirit, as the gift of prophecy or miracles was so. It was a simple process of thought; but it was very useful to me. And it is strictly just; for as nothing but Omnipotence could have created an insect or an atom, as well as an orb or an angel, nothing but the Holy Spirit could turn the heart to seek its happiness in the holy salvation of God; for this is utterly unnatural and abhorrent to man, and, therefore, the effect of Divine grace, wherever and however it is produced. Reflection, and especially afflictions, may, indeed, work a very considerable change of character, and drive men to pray earnestly for a time; but they do not sweetly *draw* to prayer, nor really endear it long. There is a mighty difference between the kind of help which they, when alone, give in prayer, and that which the Holy Spirit gives. The prayers extorted by afflic- tion are chiefly for deliverance from it, or support under it. When they regard above all things the *sanctified* use of it, there is a higher power than afflic- tion operating on the mind. The Holy Spirit is help- ing mightily, when they regard a change of heart more than a change of condition—an interest in and con- formity to Christ, more than temporal deliverance. Oh! there is no better proof of " having the Spirit," than that we would rather suffer than sin ; rather be the prisoners of Providence than the votaries of vice or the world !

All this might have been stated at once, and thus you would have escaped whatever agitation the former class of remarks occasioned. If, however, you are beginning to recover your composure, you will soon stand higher and firmer than ever you did, upon " the ministration of the Spirit." My object was to bring the question of " having the Spirit," to an issue ; for whilst it is taken for granted, or left unsettled, it is impossible to " walk or pray in the Spirit." Many leave it in suspense from year to year, and are thus all their life-long subject to the bondage of uncertainty. They cannot come to a conclusion upon their own state by a hasty glance ; and they do not go fully into the question. They are afraid to decide, and unwilling to examine. They mean well, but they think little. They are sincere, but they are also superficial. The consequence is, they seldom know what to think of their own case. Now, how much better, and in fact easier, it is to go thoroughly into the subject, until we ascertain whether or not we are partakers of the Spirit! One thorough examination of the question would save you from a thousand embarrassments in after life.

CHAPTER VI.

NTIRE and eternal "fellowship" with God and the Lamb is the perfection of the bliss of heaven. The fellowship of the saints with all the "innumerable company of angels," must be delightful; and the fellowship of the saints with each other still more pleasing, because more natural: but the fellowship of both with God, must exceed, infinitely, all the other social enjoyments of heaven. To see Him as He is, to hear Him speak, to speak with God face to face, as a man doth with his friend, must be joy "full of glory." And then—this communion with God will be eternal and universal in heaven. All will enjoy it equally, both as to degree and duration. Oh, no wonder that all must be *holy* in order to share such fellowship with God! An unholy spirit could not enjoy it, even if admitted into it. What God shows and says of Himself from the throne, to pure spirits, could only mortify and confound impure spirits.

Every look of unveiled Godhead would wither their hearts, and every word sting their consciences, just in proportion as the looks were lovely and the words kind; because the unholy would feel through all their soul that these smiles and assurances were not meant for them. Thus heaven itself would be a hell to beings who loved sin and disliked holiness.

Now, as perfect holiness is essential to fellowship with God in heaven, so the love and pursuit of holiness are essential to fellowship with Him on earth. "If I regard iniquity in my heart," said David, "the Lord will not hear me." "If we say that we have fellowship with Him," said John, "and walk in darkness, we lie, and do not the truth." Walking with God, and walking in darkness (that is, in secret or in open sin) are utterly incompatible. They never were combined, and never can be. The appearance and pretence of devotional communion with God may be combined with bad habits, so as to deceive the world, and the Church too; but the *pretender* himself is no more deceived by his own dexterity than God is. He cannot lie to himself, however he may impose on others, or elude detection. The father of lies cannot lie to himself: much less can his most expert children dupe their own consciences completely or through life.

It is supposed, I am aware, that the self-deception of the heart is so very great, that even a *sensualist* may flatter himself with the hope of salvation, and bring himself to believe that sin cannot harm him.

But, although some men have said so, and, no doubt, thought so in their own case, for a time, it remains yet to be proved that any man has *died* under this delusion, or even lived very long under it. Men of this stamp do not pass through life without checks. Reverses of some kind overtake them sooner or later ; and when "the mighty hand of God" is upon them, its pressure soon undeceives themselves, even if they continue to deceive others. These remarks apply, of course, only to those who profess themselves to be the people of God, notwithstanding their vices. Men utterly ignorant of the doctrines of grace, or indifferent about religion, may both live and die flattering themselves with the hope of safety ; but flaming professors, who are vicious, cannot carry their false security into the valley of the shadow of death. The first sweep of the swellings of Jordan wrecks their peace.

Gross vice is not, however, the only "darkness" in which no fellowship with God can be obtained. Any allowed sin will interrupt it, and any evil habit prevent it. Fellowship with God is not understood where this is not believed and felt. If, indeed, fellowship with God meant no more than freedom or fervour in prayer, there might be something of this felt at times, even by very inconsistent professors ; for they are overcome occasionally both by fear and hope, and thus drawn into something very like the spirit of real devotion. But, however they or others may call these meltings of the heart, communion with God, they are not so.

Even the delight they feel in prayer at such times is not so, even when the prayers of *such* men are both sincere and fervent, they are not fellowship with God.

There are many popular mistakes upon this subject, which require to be cleared up, for the sake of consistent, as well as of inconsistent, professors. The general opinion of both seems to be—that communion with God consists chiefly in *enjoyment* at the sacrament, and during secret prayer. And by enjoyment they mean sweet thoughts and tender feelings, arising from clear views of the love of God, and of the glory of the Saviour. When these things touch their heart, so as to melt them, they rejoice in having fellowship with God. But when they do not feel thus, they say that they have had no communion with Him.

Now, in the case of a *consistent* follower of the Saviour, the first conclusion is quite true ; his delight at the sacrament and in the closet is real fellowship with God and the Lamb. But his second conclusion may be quite untrue. The want of such enjoyment is not, necessarily, the want of fellowship with God, or with the Saviour. It may even be a higher and holier degree of it than what we call enjoyment is. Oh, yes ! when the soul is sunk in the dust of humility and self-abasement, and filled to overflowing with grief, and shame, and hatred and loathing of sin ; and so absorbed in feeling the necessity and desirableness of holiness, that it can think of nothing else at the time,—then there is more real fellowship with God and the Lamb, than when the soul can hardly contain its joys ; for this deep hatred of sin, and this deep love of holiness, are more in harmony with the mind of God than any raptures are. For what is fellowship with God, but *fellow* principles and feelings to His own ?

Such being the sober facts of the case, it is self-evident that whatever an *inconsistent* professor enjoys at the sacrament, or in secret prayer, it is not the fellowship with God and the Lamb. They hate sin. It is " the abominable thing " which their "soul hateth." Whoever, therefore, loves sin, so as to " walk " in it, is at open *variance* with God, instead of having fellowship with Him ; and at variance with God on a point which God never will yield nor alter. He will bear with weaknesses, and overlook infirmities, and even forgive, in answer to prayer, the sins of those who hate sin, and are conscientiously trying to follow holiness : but with the man who loves sin, and lives in it, God will hold no fellowship. "What fellowship hath Christ with Belial ? " None. And it is equally true that Belial (a wicked man) hath none with Christ, whatever he may think or pretend.

These hints prove that there are serious mistakes prevalent upon this subject. Inconsistent professors call that fellowship with God, which wants the very first and fundamental principle of all communion with Him. That principle is—love to what God loves most —HOLINESS ; and hatred to what God hates most— SIN. Where this principle is not in the heart, there is not, there cannot be, any fellowship with God. There may be fits of prayer without it, and flashes of enjoyment without it, and occasional meltings of heart without it; but no fellowship. It is essential, in order to that, that we have some measure of feeling with God on the points where He feels most. Were this well understood, and habitually remembered, by those who combine a profession of religion with loved and allowed sin, they would soon become as much afraid of what they call their " sweet seasons" of enjoyment, as they are now of being *detected* in their secret sins. For, nothing is more ominous or alarming than a state of mind which can *set off* fits of devotion against habits of sensuality, intemperance, lying, or dishonesty. The man who can salve up the wounds of his conscience under such habits, is really *searing* his conscience, with the hottest " iron " that Satan heats. " If we say that we have fellowship with Him, and walk in darkness, we lie."

" But if we walk in the light as He is in the light, we have mutual fellowship with Him." Walking in the light is both the rule and the condition of communion with God. It is itself practical fellowship with God, and leads to that devotional fellowship which consists in the sensible enjoyment of the Divine presence. But it may be said, " Walking in the light as God is in the light," seems to be impossible : " God is light, and in Him is *no darkness* at all ! " how, then, can any one walk in the light as He is in the light? This objection is not so formidable as it appears at first sight. The apostle's object is, not to demand perfection, but to establish a perfect rule of conduct. The angels cannot walk in the light to all the extent which God is in the light; but they act upon His principles, copy His example, and cultivate His spirit. They adopt no lower, nor any other, standard of holiness. Now, although we cannot equal angels in walking in the light, we can, like them, make God our example; and although we cannot come up to that example, we can avoid coming down to an inferior one. Perfection is, indeed, impossible in this world: but it is not impossible to make use of a perfect model or rule of conduct. Let us, therefore, consider how "God is in the light."

Now, in Him there is none of the darkness of *insincerity.* God never says one thing, and *means* another; never professes friendship, when He feels none; never employs fraud or flattery to gain his ends. All this, however, is common in the world; and, because it is common, God puts Himself forward as the authoritative example of sincerity to all who desire fellowship with Him. He will not allow us to make any man, nor any angel, the standard of our sincerity; but insists upon it, that we look to Himself as our model. Now, this is not impossible. It is, in fact, the easiest of all the rules of speaking or acting, to set the Lord before us. The moment we realise to ourselves His sincerity, we see at a glance, how He would speak and act; and thus see how we ought to conduct the business and intercourse of life. No man can be at a loss what to say, in any given case, if he is determined to be sincere as God is sincere. This rule would put an end to all shuffling, equivocating, and colouring, as well as to all lying and pretence. This virtue of *godlike* sincerity or integrity would also be its own reward, even if it had no connection with the promise of the Divine presence. Sterling and uniform uprightness, in word and deed, commands or wins the homage of all men ; and, what is infinitely better, it secures, to a believer, joy and peace in believing. The God of truth marks His approbation of all who walk in the light of truth, by lifting upon them the light of His own countenance. He "manifests" Himself to them in a way that He "does not" to the insincere and the half-honest. The fact is, God regulates His fellowship with His professed friends, by the same general principle on which we regulate our own fellow ship with our acquaintances. We avoid, as much as possible, all intimacy with the double-minded, and the tricky, and the false-tongued. We make them feel by our manner, that we cannot rely on them, nor ac with them. They sit upon *thorns* whilst in our com pany. And whatever be their profession of religion such persons find a similar reception from God, both at the sacrament and in the closet. There, too, they sit or kneel upon thorns.

Again : in God there is none of the darkness o *pride*. He is majestic, but condescending also. A His dignity is as amiable as it is exalted. He is no a respecter of persons, nor ashamed to own the poores

sheep or lamb of the good Shepherd's flock. He
readily and equally holds fellowship with all His people
of equal character, however unequal may be their rank
in life, or their range of talent. Now, it is impossible
for believers to imitate God in this condescension and
impartiality. We may walk in the light of humility,
as He does in the light of condescension. It is necessary to do so, if we would obtain fellowship with God
in our closets, or at the sacrament ; for He will not
countenance any believer who is ashamed to own, as
brethren, the poorest of the flock : but as sure as he
declines fellowship with them, he loses fellowship with
God. "The first" in rank in a Church is always "the
last" in devotional enjoyment, whenever he is a con-
sequential man. God keeps just as far off from him
as he himself keeps far off from his brethren. Such a
man is as seldom upon the mount of communion as he
is seldom in the company of the Church. His distance, and airs, and self-importance, are thus their own
punishment. They may not, indeed, draw down upon
himself the contempt of his brethren : they may bear
his high hand and brook his haughty spirit ; but God
will do neither. The proud are an abomination to the
Lord, and He beholdeth them afar off ; and, although
He does not always punish them in their person or
property, He invariably withdraws and withholds from
them the sense of His gracious presence. None are so
much neglected by God as those who neglect the
people of God. There is no light in the countenance
of God for the man who darkens his own countenance

when he looks upon "men of low estate" in the Church. But, on the other hand, when pious men of rank or wealth are humble, affable, and impartial; and when they employ their influence to promote the welfare of the Church, none are more honoured by God, either at the sacrament or in the closet. They are, emphatically, the men " whom the King delighteth to honour."

Again: in God there is none of the darkness of *imprudence.* He does not speak rashly, nor act without deliberation. He promises nothing but what He can perform, and engages in nothing which can involve His character in the least. And here, also, He is the example to them that fear Him. We cannot, indeed, imitate the wisdom of God so as to become infallible in our judgment, or unerring in our management; but we can think before we speak; we can deliberate before we decide; we can stand aloof from hazardous and questionable undertakings; we can avoid giving pledges which we are not likely to redeem; we can keep clear of those habits which weaken the understanding and pervert the conscience. Oh, were all the professed followers of Christ doing all that they could do, in guiding themselves and their affairs " with discretion," how much more fellowship with God many of them might enjoy! But, if a man contract debts beyond his means of payment, or launch out in business upon mere credit without capital; or involve himself and his friends by rash speculation; or give in to the *sottish* system of transacting business at taverns; or so entangle himself with pledges as to be for ever at his "wits' end" for new shifts and excuses—that man cannot have communion with God either in the sanctuary or the closet. His closet, indeed, will seldom see him. And if he continue to visit the sanctuary, and pretend to be *comforted* there, whilst persisting in this course, his case is ominous indeed! Comfort! There is no comfort in the Gospel for the dishonest or the drunken, but the comfort that arises from the fact —that the blood of Christ can cleanse from all sin, and grace teach them to "live soberly and honestly" in the world. Any comfort which does not stop crime is a curse. But, on the other hand, the man who brings both the Gospel and the law to bear upon all his affairs, to regulate his expenditure, to form his promises, to moderate his desires, to bind his soul to the example of his Saviour—that man will not pray without comfort, nor communicate without enjoyment. Others may pretend, but He will "truly" say, My "fellowship is with the Father, and with his Son Jesus Christ."

Again : in God there is none of the darkness of *passion.* He is "slow to anger," and never angry without a just cause. It is not mistakes nor trifles that He takes offence at. And even when He is justly angry, He does not abandon the offender at once. Thus God is "in the light;" and in all this He is our example. "Walking in the light as He is in the light," in this respect, is essential to fellowship with Him, for the God of love will not countenance an angry man. Such is His aversion to all strife between brethren, that He commands the offender to leave the altar and the gift too, until he is reconciled to his brother. He even suspends forgiveness upon forgiving. But even if this were not the case, nor God to hide His countenance from the angry, anger itself would disable us from seeing the face of God. It is physically, as well as morally, impossible to pray in a passion.

Well might Jeremy Taylor say "Prayer is the daughter of charity, and the sister of meekness ; and he that prays to God in an angry spirit is like him who retires into a battle to meditate, and sets up his closet in the out-quarters of an enemy, and chooses a frontier garrison to be wise in. Anger is a perfect alienation of the mind from prayer, and therefore is contrary to that attention which presents our prayers in a *right line* to heaven. For so I have seen a lark rising from his bed of grass, and soaring upwards, singing as he rises, and hopes to get to heaven and climb above the clouds. But the poor bird was beaten back with the loud sighing of an eastern wind, and his motion made irregular and inconstant ; descending more, at every breath of the tempest, than he could recover by the libration and frequent weighing of his wings ; till the little creature was forced to sit down and pant, and stay till the storm was over ; and then it made a prosperous flight, and did rise and sing as if it had learned music and motion from an angel, as he passed sometimes through the air, about his ministeries here below.

" So is the prayer of a good man when anger raises a tempest and overcomes him. Then his prayer was broken, and his thoughts were troubled, and his words went up towards a cloud ; and his thoughts pulled them back again, and made them without intention. And the good man sighs for his infirmity ; but must be content to lose the prayer ; and he must recover it when his anger is removed, and his spirit is becalmed, and made even as the brow of Jesus, and smooth like the heart of God : and then it ascends to heaven upon the wings of the holy dove, and dwells with God, till it returns like the useful bee, laden with a blessing and the dew of heaven."

CHAPTER VII.

A DEVOTIONAL SPIRIT ESSENTIAL TO THE ENJOYMENT OF THE PROMISES.

OTHING is more obvious than that eternal things are not seen in their true light by the generality of mankind. Men could not act as they do if they saw eternal realities in the light of revelation. Accordingly, whenever any great truth shines out upon them with unusual clearness, they change, or resolve to change, their line of conduct. They can neither act nor feel as usual, while that truth is before them in its brightness and solemnity. It is master whilst it can keep on the meridian of their minds. It is, therefore, self-evident that if all the great truths of the Gospel were vividly and habitually before their minds, a change of conduct and feeling would be the inevitable effect. No man could go on in sin or sloth who saw, as in sunlight, the fatal and eternal consequences of neglecting the great salvation. No man could " halt between two opinions," who saw the two worlds, Heaven and Hell, as God has exhibited them in His own Word. They are not seen in His ".light," by any one who trifles with them. It is the light of custom—of convenience—of passion, that is upon eternal things, whenever they are unfelt or uninfluential. The indifference which some manifest, and the indecision which marks others, is, therefore, the exact measure of their *spiritual* blindness. They may not be ignorant, but what they know they have not weighed nor searched out for themselves. Their knowledge has been forced upon them by circumstances, or picked up by accident and at second-hand. It is not the fruit of searching the Scriptures, nor of serious consideration, nor of secret prayer. They have just light enough to render their indifference and indecision highly criminal and utterly inexcusable ; but not light enough to terminate them, nor even to keep them from growing worse. For it is quite possible for an undecided man to become insensible, and for a heedless man to become reckless, whilst he only sees the truth of God in the light of the world. In that light it has little authority and less glory. It has not the force of truth upon the heart or the character. Accordingly, whilst men content themselves with holding the truth in the vague and general forms in which it is afloat in the world, and merely fall in with public opinion, instead of forming their own opinions from the Word of God, they may remain heedless and heartless for any length of time. The Word of God itself must be used as the Word of God, before it can prove the power of God unto salvation.

F

It is, therefore, no wonder that so many, who seem to know so much about the soul and eternity, should yet trifle with both. For what is there in their knowledge to prevent trifling? It relates, indeed, to grand and solemn truths ; but not to these truths as they stand in the Bible, nor as they flow from the lips of Jehovah, but as they float in public opinion. And when thus separated from God Himself, and from His "lively oracles," they cannot make men wise unto salvation.

If these hints explain, in any measure, the carelessness and indecision of the multitude, they will also explain many of the relapses of the serious. Truth has not always the *force* of truth upon them. They revere it, and love it, and wish to remain under its influence. And at times it is sweeter to their taste than honey, or the honey-comb. But, somehow, they often lose their relish for it. Even their *knowledge*, as well as their enjoyment of the glorious Gospel, fades away insensibly from time to time. They lose both the sight and the sense of truths which have made their hearts sing for joy, even in the day of adversity.

Now, all this surprises as well as grieves them. They cannot always account for it. It seems so strange, as well as melancholy, that truths which had been often before the mind in light and loveliness, in power and glory, should ever disappear or become dim ! If they had not been loved whilst they shone in beauty, or not improved whilst they captivated the heart, their eclipse would explain itself. But they have become dark and distant, even when we were not conscious of misimproving them; they have vanished away, even whilst we were fondly calculating that we could never again forget or misunderstand them.

All this, however, is not so strange as it is lamentable. It arises, in many instances, from ceasing to "search the Scriptures" as we did, whilst we were absorbed with the question, "What shall I do to be saved?" When we can answer this question to our own satisfaction, we are prone to relax in our attention to the word of God. Having discovered our way and welcome to the cross, we do not feel the same necessity for continuing our inquiries. And the whole matter seems so plain, and so pleasing, that we take for granted that we can never lose sight of it. Thus we come to put our clear views in the room of the Scriptures, and begin to draw upon them, instead of continuing to "draw water from the wells of salvation." The consequence is, that our clearest views of the Gospel soon become indistinct. Hence the necessity of habitual attention to the word of God, however clear or copious our knowledge of it may be. We never can safely dispense with it, whatever be our experience or progress in the Divine life. It must be "the light of our feet," until they stand on the sea of glass before the throne.

It is not, however, a formal use of the Scriptures that will maintain, in brightness and power, those views of Divine truth which were acquired by a *devotional* use of the Scriptures. We were blending much fervent prayer with our frequent reading of them, when we first discovered the way of salvation for ourselves. We pondered and prayed over the word of God at the same time. Like David, we were upon our knees when we said, " In thy light shall we see light." We both recognised and realised the presence of God with His own oracles; and with something of the solemnity, and much of the sincerity, of the high-priest, when he went within the veil, we opened our Bibles, saying, " I will hear what God the Lord will speak." In a word, our searching the Scriptures was truly a devotional exercise, when we obtained that view of the Gospel which relieved our consciences and calmed our spirits.

This experimental fact demands and deserves the utmost attention. Remember! you were not only thoughtful and watchful, but prayerful also, when the great salvation opened upon your mind, in its own native glory and simplicity. Whether the discovery was made by you in the sanctuary or in the closet, it was intimately connected with prayer, and however clearly it shone in the sanctuary, it shone still clearer when you retired to pray over it. You saw and felt then that this " marvellous light " was both the answer and the effect of prayer.

Such being the real facts of the case, it is self-evident that any decline of *prayerful* attention to the word of God must dim the clearness, and diminish the sweetness, of all those principles and promises which you first discovered, when in a truly devotional spirit. The decay of that spirit must darken them. They were first seen when you were living very "near" to God; and, therefore, all receding from that nearness must involve a proportionate losing sight of them. In a word, whatever we saw and enjoyed in the Gospel, whilst we were very prayerful, can only be kept sight of, so as to be enjoyed, by continuing prayerful.

This general principle is of universal application. It applies particularly to the enjoyment of that "good hope through grace," JUSTIFICATION by faith alone. This is a truth which the *prayerless* cannot enjoy, however well they may understand it. Very few of them do understand it at all, or even notice it. As a *peculiarity* of the Gospel, however, it is understood by some of the prayerless. They can argue about it, and prove it from Scripture, and point out the preachers and writers who garble or encumber the doctrine. Some of this class have neither mercy nor patience for any man who seems to see less clearly than themselves, that believing is faith, and that faith justifies the soul. They can demonstrate all this—to his confusion, and to his condemnation too! To hear them declaiming and denouncing thus, one would imagine that they *enjoyed* the doctrine as much as they understood it. This, however, is not the case. Accordingly, the moment they are brought to the point by the pointed question, "Are you justified by your belief of the truth?" they dare not say that they are. The consciousness of being prayerless, and averse to secret prayer, shuts their lips at once. They may continue to argue the general principle, and even go on to show that its truth is in no wise affected by their uncertainty; but beyond this they cannot proceed. They see clearly that believers are justified by believing; but they see as clearly that it is not safe to reckon their own prayerless belief, faith.

Now, what the prayerless cannot enjoy, the serious dare not enjoy when they cease to be prayerful. The conclusion : "I believe on the Saviour, and therefore am justified for His sake," cannot be drawn so as to be satisfactory to the mind, when the heart is not right with God in the closet. It may, indeed, be drawn as a logical syllogism ; but it will only have the effect of dry logic. It will not heal the wounds, nor hush the fears, of the conscience, whilst conscience must confess to itself, that secret devotion is neglected or hurried over. Indeed, in such a state of mind, justification by faith alone will appear, at times, a doubtful doctrine, or faith will be supposed to mean much more than the cordial belief of the Gospel : and thus the man to whom the whole matter was equally plain, pleasing, and valid, whilst he was devotional in his spirit and habits, may come to doubt and distrust the whole matter ; or, at least, to be unable to derive any comfort from it. For when the heart is estranged from God, or sunk into cold formality in prayer, salvation by faith will appear just as difficult as salvation by works.

These difficulties are, I am aware, felt at times, by

many of the prayerful. But in general those who feel them most have never clearly understood the doctrine of justification by faith, nor perceived that prayer is the best expression of faith. They have either heard a misty Gospel or misunderstood the preacher, and thus have always been at a loss on the subject. But their difficulties would be removed at once if the matter were fully explained to them ; because to their devotional spirit it would commend itself as the truth of God. Whereas, in the case of those who once understood and enjoyed the doctrine, but have lost the spirit of prayer, no explanation of it will remove their difficulties, unless at the same time it restore that spirit. The sober fact is, that the loss of a devotional spirit operates, in reference to the Gospel, just as the loss of a *mental* faculty does in reference to the affairs of life. Whilst the alienation lasts, the judgments of the mind are not sound nor consistent ; things do not appear in their true light, or are not applied to their right purpose. In the same way, therefore, that a sane mind is essential for the wise management of human affairs, so is a devotional spirit to the enjoyment of Divine truth. Indeed, a dislike of prayer is a species of moral insanity. He is not " in his right mind " towards God or towards himself who has not begun to pray ; nor is he who has ceased to pray fervently. Accordingly, the first thing which the Spirit of God does, both in converting a sinner, and in restoring a backslider, is to bring them to their knees in secret, to seek God with all their heart.

The general principle of these hints is equally applicable to the enjoyment of the spirit of ADOPTION. The witness of the Holy Spirit with our spirit, that we are the children of God, will not survive the death of prayer. The spirit of adoption is essentially and invariably devotional. It "*cries*—Abba, Father." Accordingly, when this filial cry ceases in the closet, the sense of sonship is soon gone from the heart. No wonder! For if it be often difficult, and sometimes almost impossible, even when we are most prayerful, to cherish the hope that we are the children of God, it must be felt to be sheer presumption to do so, when the heart is estranged from prayer.

I do not mean, of course, that sonship is disannulled or disproved by a decay of devotional feeling and habits; but I do mean—that such a decay is, whilst it lasts, fatal to the conscious enjoyment of sonship. The *logic* of the doctrine will not keep up the hope of the fact. It is perfectly true that whoever is a believer is fully warranted to consider himself a child of God; and it is equally true that relapses in devotion do not prove a man to be an absolute unbeliever; but neither fact will meet our case whilst we are undevotional, because in that state we are not believing with the heart. Faith is not dead when the spirit of prayer is lost; but it is such a *faint*, when it ceases to breathe prayer, that neither reason nor conscience dare venture to argue from its bare existence that we are the sons and daughters of the Lord God Almighty."

We may not, indeed, give up all hope of sonship, even when things are at this low ebb in our closet. The mind will look, and the heart will linger over the fact, that it is "by faith," sonship is obtained. And we may also cling to the weak vestiges of our former believing, as evidences of having "the root of the matter" within us still. And we may try to draw the conclusion, that all is safe, although much be far wrong. But this will not do; it does not satisfy the heart, however it may blunt the stings of conscience. Our common sense frowns upon the paltry stratagem of proving our safety by a logical quibble, whilst the great body of our feelings are in a bad state ! The sad difference between these desperate graspings at *indirect* means of comfort, and our former calm hold of the cross, whilst we were prayerful, alarms us and shames us. We had then no temptation, because no occasion, to have recourse to a reckless logic, which tries to circumvent or evade God, by holding Him to the *letter* of some promise, the spirit and design of which we disregard. Oh, nothing is so pitiable an expedient as this ! It is contemptible and impious when the heart is estranged from God, and averse to prayer, to clutch at, and cling to, some subterfuge which, like a flaw in an indictment, is a mere evasion. And yet this is, alas ! the use which many make of some of the doctrines of grace. But how much better and easier is it to set the whole matter right, by a prompt and penitential return to the throne of grace ! Half the thought usually spent in juggling the conscience would suffice to bring and bind it over to its old habits of watchfulness and prayer. And these *will* maintain the spirit of adoption wherever the doctrine of adoption is understood. The substance of that doctrine is, that whoever has welcomed the Saviour to his heart for holy purposes, is both warranted and welcome to reckon himself a child of God. It is his *duty*, as well as his privilege, to believe his own sonship. And the witness of the Holy Spirit with his spirit, that he is born of God, is, amongst other things, a witness to the truth of this *revealed* fact.

The general principle of these hints applies equally to the enjoyment of the doctrine of the FINAL PERSE-VERANCE of believers. Now, that men, concerned about the eternal salvation of their souls, should cling with a tenacious grasp to a doctrine which makes salvation sure, is only what might be expected. There is so much treachery in the heart, so many snares in the world, and such depths and wiles in the temptations of Satan, that I cannot, for my own part, understand the conduct of those who deny the doctrine of final perseverance. Many of them are too holy and too humble to think seriously that they can " endure to the end " by their own strength. They manifest in their prayers that they feel them-selves dependent upon Him who " began the good work," for the on-carrying of it from day to day. And if they do, indeed, calculate, with any certainty, on being kept *by the day* from falling, they might just as well calculate by the year, or for life ; for they are only subdividing the promise in appearance, without subverting the principle in reality.   But whether for the day, the year, or for life, the calculation, if made to any purpose, must be made in a devotional spirit. As in the former cases, the dry logic of the doctrine will not maintain the hope of the promise.   It cannot do so in any sober mind ; for the promise is, that He who began the good work will carry it on :—of course, therefore, carry it on in its *goodness*.   It is not, therefore, *that* work which is going on, when a devotional spirit is going off.

CHAPTER VIII.

DEVOTIONAL PREPARATION FOR THE SANCTUARY.

IF the house of God be, indeed, "the gate of heaven," it demands and deserves from us far more than regular, or even reverential, attendance. We ought to prepare for it, as well as to repair to it. We ought to be "in the Spirit," as well as in our place, on the Lord's day; for the house of God is the gate of heaven only to the "spiritually minded." It is not such a gate of heaven as that which John saw in Patmos—so wide and so open that he had only to look, in order to behold the throne of God and the mansions of glory. It is rather such a gate as the types were to the Saviour before His coming, or as the prophecies are to futurity: solemn, but shadowy; direct, but dim; so that if our minds be not spiritual when we enter it, we shall see but little, and enjoy less, of the heaven to which it leads.

Accordingly, we have found, when we have come into the house of God altogether unprepared, that it was anything but the gate of heaven to our souls. It has been the gate of sleep, or the gate of weariness to us, when we have entered it prayerless; and we have felt it to be almost the gate of hell when all its ordinances poured fire into our consciences, and fear into our hearts. And this they have done, when our utter want of relish for them has forced upon us the awful suspicion that we were surely *hardening* under the Gospel!

These are melancholy and humiliating confessions. They ought, however, to be thus publicly made, that we may be shamed out of those habits which bring on such states of mind; and that we may see and feel the necessity of due preparation for the house of God. For it may be to us the gate of heaven, if we come to it in a right spirit and with proper motives. Now we have much need that it should be so to us. For if the house of God do not fix our minds on eternal things, no other house is likely to bring us under the powers of the world to come. The house of mourning, by its gloom and by its silence, renders us solemn and thoughtful whilst we are in it; but its deep influence is not lasting: it lessens every day after the funeral, and soon subsides entirely. And in the world, although there are events for ever occurring which ought to burn in upon our souls the conviction that " this is not our rest,"—this, alas! is not the lesson we learn from them! This world, with all its cares and crosses, does not, by its own influence, throw our thoughts direct or often upon the world to come. Even when we ourselves are the sufferers, such is the tendency of our minds, that we are inclined to turn our trials into excuses for the neglect of the great salvation ;—so that unless the house of God furnish an antidote to these plagues of our hearts, they are sure to ruin us. We are, therefore, deeply interested and obligated to form and maintain such devotional habits of preparation for the sanctuary, that its "waters" may be for us, from Sabbath to Sabbath, cleansing, healing, and refreshing. David felt the necessity of this, and never trusted his principles of love or relish for Zion to their own vitality or unaided influence ; but prayed habitually : "O send out Thy light and Thy truth: let them lead me, let them bring me unto Thy holy hill and to Thy tabernacles. Then will I go unto the altar of God, unto God, my exceeding joy." It was thus that David found the house of God to be the gate of heaven to his soul.

Whenever the benefits of the sanctuary are thus strongly stated, and preparation for it thus solemnly enforced, you naturally, and not improperly, advert in your own minds to the character and preaching of the minister of that sanctuary which you attend. And you ought to "take heed" *whom* you hear, and *what* you hear, as well as "how you hear." It is as much your duty to quit a minister who is not a man of God, and to shun a ministry which shuns to declare the whole counsel of God, as it is to attend the house of God. Your love to Zion is lukewarm, if you countenance a bad man or false doctrine in Zion. Hearers have it, however, in their power to make both a good man and good preaching much better. For, if both are worthy of esteem, even whilst his people are not very prayerful, or whilst only a few of them are so, what would his spirit and sermons be, were he sure that the great body of his charge came from their closets to the sanctuary?

You have perhaps said, when you heard of the preaching of Whitefield, Romaine, and Spencer, Why do not our ministers preach with their unction and energy? One reason is, that far fewer pray for us than the number who prayed for them. Whitefield was borne up and borne through by the high and sweet consciousness, that underneath him were the wings of the secret and family prayers of thousands. He had Aarons and Hurs to hold up his hands upon every mount to Amalek, where he unfurled the standard of the cross. Under such circumstances he could not, and no good man could, be cold or tame in his preaching.

It may be said, in answer to this, " that Whitefield, by his own devotional spirit and example, created the prayerfulness which thus inspired and sustained him." And to a great extent this is true. But " prayer was made for him," not only by his own converts, but by all who loved and longed for the conversion of souls. He knew this, and " watched for souls," as one who must give account.

Now, something, yea, much of this, you may promote by a prayerful regard to your own profiting; for if you consult your own spiritual benefit, your minister is sure to be benefited. A praying people will make a preaching minister, as much by their prayers for *themselves* as by what they offer for him. And in this obvious way: While the consciousness that he has not been forgotten at the mercy-seat will soothe his spirit, the consciousness that you have been *alone* with God, and are come from communing with God and the Lamb, will rouse his spirit to meet your spirit, so as to *mingle* with it in all its holy aspirations. He will feel, through all his soul, that a devotional people cannot be edified by an undevotional minister,—that a sermon unbaptized by prayer will betray itself and him too, amongst the prayerful; and that no dexterity in speaking will mask heartlessness in thinking. Thus he will have, in your devotional character, a check upon his own; and his own, thus kept on the alert, will re-act upon yours, in a similar way.

Besides, if your errand to the house of God be a *spiritual* one, you cannot expect to succeed without trying, at least, to be "in the Spirit on the Lord's day," before you go out. It should not depend upon the morning prayer, or the morning sermon, of the minister, whether you shall be in a good or bad frame of mind during the Sabbath. They may, indeed, have occasionally broken up a bad frame of mind, and been, unexpectedly, the means of restoring your soul from its wanderings; but whenever they have been instrumental in this way, you have been made to feel deeply, at the time, that such sovereign *lifts* were fraught with reproof, as well as with revival. You never were unexpectedly quickened in the sanctuary, without being cut to the heart, by the consciousness that you might have been restored sooner, if you had not restrained prayer before God. Accordingly, your first resolution, when thus brought again to your "right mind," was, that you would not let things go wrong again between you and God, by coming prayerless or heartless to the house of God. I remind you of this fact, that you may feel that you have no reason to expect to see His glory in the sanctuary, unless you have prayed at home—"I beseech Thee, show me Thy glory." Whatever is worth *finding* in His house, is worth *seeking* in your own closet. It is therefore presumption, if not high insult, to expect the Divine presence or blessing in Zion, if we neglect to pray for them before we come to Zion. If we would feed upon its "green pastures," or be refreshed by its "still waters," we must, like David, pray—"O send out Thy light and Thy truth; let them lead me, let them guide me to Thy holy hill."

It is much easier to enforce this rule than to endear it. It may, however, be commended, as well as commanded; for your own comfort is inseparably connected with its observance. Now you know, by experience, that it is a wretched post to sit in the house of God listening to promises which you cannot lay hold on for yourselves; looking at prospects of heaven, which you dare not realise; hearing of sweet feelings, which you have lost! Nothing is more painful than to see the wells of salvation overflowing with the water of life, and feel averse or unable to drink. The fabled cup of Tantalus is nothing to this, when the soul feels, at the same time, its own value, and cannot forget the solemnities of eternity. Well, whatever there be in all this that is humiliating or painful, it commends, as well as enforces, thoughtful and prayerful preparation for the sanctuary. For you do not, you cannot, wish to spend Sabbath after Sabbath thus cold and comfortless. Only think of a *year* of such Sabbaths ! No communion with God—no witness of the Spirit—no foretastes of heaven—no growth in grace—no peace of conscience—no holy liberty of soul in prayer or praise? Can you bear the idea of this? If not, what is to prevent the reality, if sloth or sleep be allowed to waste the Sabbath morning? For, be assured, God will not humour our indolence by comforting us under it. The arm of the Lord will not "awake" to uphold or protect us, if we sleep, when we ought to be up and calling on it to awake for our help. We have found, by experience, that this is only too true.

Happily, however, this is not the whole of our experience. We have found, too, at times, that the "glorious things" spoken of Zion are true. "As we have heard, so have we seen in the city of God." The house of God has been, indeed, the very gate of heaven to us. It was so when the great salvation first opened upon us in its greatness—when the glories of the cross first awoke our wonder—when we first saw our own way and welcome to the refuge set before us in the Gospel—when we felt the first rising of a hope full of immortality, and, with adoring, but speechless gratitude, wept out the weighty sentiment, " Why me —why me, Lord?" The Sabbath was not a weariness then, nor the ordinances of the sanctuary tedious. We felt as if we could have taken an eternity of these hallowed hours and emotions. ·

I appeal to you for the truth of this statement. I must do more :—Was your *business* or your *family* neglected or injured at all, whilst your soul was thus absorbed with the glories of salvation? Had your wife, your children, your tradesmen, your servants, reason to complain of your conduct or spirit, whilst you were thus happy in religion? O, no !—this good hope through grace exalted all that was good in your character or temper, and brought under strong restraints all that was bad in both. Yes ; and whatever relapse there has been in either since, has risen, in no small degree, from the decay of that good hope. " For whosoever hath his hope in Christ purifieth himself even as He is pure," whilst it is devotionally maintained.

It may be, however, that you suspect it to be impossible to maintain a settled hope of salvation. You may have found it decline and shake, even whilst your general character remained firm ; and thus you have been led to think that, do what you would, you cannot keep it up. Now, on the supposition that there is much truth in all this, see what it proves, viz., that if the ordinances and the fellowship, the checks and charms of the house of God, *lose* their influence over you, you may be a lost man in the hour of trial and temptation! For if you have not hope enough to fortify you against them, you, of all men, need most to improve Divine ordinances, that their sweet influence may aid your feeble hopes. It is, therefore, at your peril, during all the week, if you come to the sanctuary hurried or heartless. For, unless you are awed or encouraged by eternal things on the Sabbath, and kept alive to the worth of your soul and the evil of sin, and kept under a deep sense of the Divine presence and authority, and held up by the counsel and example of your brethren, you cannot " stand in the evil day." And as the bare idea of apostatising, or falling, shocks you, O risk not the dread reality by coming prayerless to the house of God. Thoughtful and prayerful preparation for the sanctuary is, however, not less necessary in the case of those who enjoy some *settled* hope of eternal life. A good hope through grace can only be well maintained by acquiring " more grace." This is wanted, in order to keep before you the *grounds* of hope in their strength and glory. Any one can talk of Christ being the sole and sure foundation of all warrantable hope. Any one can argue that the love and mercy of the Divine character warrant much hope. But—to see this clearly, to feel it powerfully, to realise it for ourselves so vividly as to enjoy it, is not an easy attainment, nor, when attained, easily kept up. In fact, these realising views of the glorious Gospel fade and vanish away whenever the spirit of devotion is allowed to decline. And they *are* both dim and indistinct, on all the Sabbath mornings when you have no heart for secret prayer. Their distance from you is always the measure of your distance from God. Your hopes are just firm as the cherubim upon the mercy-seat, in proportion as you act as a priest before it. Or, if they do stand, after the spirit of prayer is fallen, they stand only as the cherubim when the glory departed—cold and naked. Thus it is that the want of a good conscience towards God or man, overthrows or overcasts a good hope through grace. And no sermon which does not set the *conscience* right, can set up, or clear up, that hope again. Accordingly, you have found, when you have came prayerless to the sanctuary, or without such praying as will bear to be *thought* of, the best sermons have failed to comfort you. You durst not take comfort from them, owing to the cutting recollection, that your heart was far from God, or not right with God at home. Whereas, when you have prayed so that your sincerity and solicitude were beyond a doubt; so that you could appeal to the Searcher of hearts as the witness of your spiritual desires; and so that it was not *unlikely* that He would meet with you, and manifest Himself to your soul in His house,— you have then found that you could " take the cup of salvation," and drink abundantly, without fear or overwhelming shame.

Oh, why should it not be always thus with you? It might be so. God is not unwilling that you should

be " joyful in the house of prayer." He has not made
it a *difficult* thing to rejoice before Him in Zion.
There is provision enough in the unsearchable riches
of Christ to make His people "shout aloud for joy."
And all that is wanted in order to bring or keep their
harps from the "willows," is *holding faith and a good
conscience,* by frequent and fervent prayer for the work
and witness of the Spirit.

Happiness in the sanctuary is not, however, the
only thing which we need. As parents, we need
grace to help us to train up our children in the nur-
ture and admonition of the Lord. And we feel that,
if we were to forsake the house of God, we not only
could not expect Him to bless our families, but that
our example might ruin them. So far we judge
aright. But we ought also to be intent upon deriving
such benefit from Divine ordinances that our parental
character may improve every Sabbath in worth and
weight. We ought never to visit the house of God
without looking at our children in the light both of
time and eternity, and praying that the means of
grace may revive and increase our love to their souls.
We, in fact, forget one grand part of our errand to
the gates of Zion, if we do not seek expressly and im-
portunately to be fitted for the duties of *home,* as well
as of public life. Every Sabbath ought to make us,
and might make us, better fathers and mothers. For
it is not necessary, in order to be so, that parental
duties should be often brought before us. Any subject, and every subject, which brings eternal things to

bear upon our hearts and consciences, will improve and confirm our parental character.

Whatever truth there is in these views of the nature and necessity of devout preparation for public worship, is of supreme importance to all those who have much to do or suffer in the world. If your Sabbaths are not made the most of, by being well prepared for and well spent, it must go very ill with your souls during the week. The bustle and cares of life, as you well know, have a desolating and hardening influence upon the heart. They sometimes almost upset the form of godliness, as well as deaden the power of it; and thus throw the mind into a state of such hurry, and confusion, and restlessness, and impatience, that it can hardly detach itself from its business and embarrassments. These even follow you to the house of God, and force themselves into your closet, and up to the sacramental table, at times. Now, if this haunting and harassing influence of the world should go farther, and get a firmer hold upon you, it may end fatally. It has placed you already upon what you feel to be the brink of a precipice which makes you almost totter. The same influence, when given way to, has drowned many in perdition, or pierced them through with many sorrows. Now, if you would stand, you must "take heed lest you fall." But it is not taking sufficient "heed," merely to maintain your attendance upon the sanctuary. That is, indeed, essential to your safety ; for God will forsake the man who forsakes His word and worship. ·That man will sink as surely as if he were to quit a ship in the midst of the ocean. More, however, is requisite than not "for-saking the assembling of ourselves together" with them who love Zion. You must strive to be "in the Spirit on the Lord's day," if you would pass unspotted or safely through the world during the week. For, if you find it to be hard work to 'possess your soul in patience," or to maintain the power of godliness, amidst the pressure of your engagements, even in those weeks which are ushered in by refreshing Sab-baths and enjoyed sacraments, it must be impossible to do so when Sabbaths and sacraments are not "times of refreshing from the presence of the Lord."

Men of business! suffer the word of exhortation. You know that the influence of the world is baneful. But, do acquaint yourselves fully with the Saviour's opinion of it. Christ never spoke of the world to His disciples, but with the most tremendous emphasis. There is nothing in all that he said of danger from Satan, more solemn than what he said of the evil of the world. The prayer he offered on Peter's behalf, when Satan desired to sift him as wheat, has not been left on record; whereas the prayer against the evil influence of the world is recorded at full length. No prayer of Christ is so long, or more fervent. He repeats the petition again and again, that His disciples may be kept from "the evil."

This is not by accident. John, who heard and recorded this prayer, evidently regarded the fact as full of special design. And that he remembered it through life, is certain from the frequency and force of his protests against the love of the world. His epistles are a solemn commentary on the Saviour's intercessory prayer. And, in the same spirit, Paul's chief practical reason for glorying only in the cross of Christ is assigned thus : "by which I am crucified unto the world, and the world unto me."

Now, you are emphatically " in the world," and can only be effectually "kept from the evil of it," by making your Sabbaths a cloud of glory, which shall encircle and enshrine the whole week with the light and warmth of devotion.

CHAPTER IX.

THE INFLUENCE OF PRAYER UPON PEACE OF MIND UNDER THE TRIALS OF LIFE.

HAT an idea Paul must have had of prayer, as an antidote to the cares of life and godliness, when he said to the Philippians, "Be careful for nothing; but in everything, by prayer and supplication, with thanksgiving, let your requests be made known unto God; and the peace of God, which passeth all understanding, shall keep your hearts and minds through Christ Jesus!" This way of disposing of our cares and anxieties is so little understood, or so much disliked, that we are inclined to doubt its efficacy in our own case; or to ask, How is it possible, in a world like this, to "be careful for nothing?" Our temporal cares are, as we think, our chief hindrances in prayer. We even turn them, at times, into excuses for the neglect of prayer; and imagine, when our cares are many and pressing, that much prayer cannot be expected from us. For, whatever influence the calamities of life may have in sending us often to our knees, the *cares* of life have a direct tendency to set aside, or shorten secret prayer. Indeed, at first sight, our ordinary cares do not seem to us to be things which prayer can remedy, but things which only time and toil can remove. Accordingly, when our temporal affairs go wrong, or our prospects darken, without exactly overwhelming us, we naturally devote to them, not a larger measure of secret prayer, but a larger portion of time and thought. It is *thinking*, not praying, that seems called for, under embarrassment and anxiety. Under heavy calamity, whether personal or domestic, we see at once, that prayer is our only resource, because God alone can deliver us ; but when we are merely vexed or plagued, we feel as if deliverance depended more upon our own good management, or upon the conduct of others, than upon the providence of God. Thus we are tempted to lessen prayer, and to increase effort, under an idea that great effort is the only remedy.

And, certainly, without effort, prayer will not prove a remedy for misfortune or embarrassment. He who does nothing but pray, when the times are bad, or his affairs trying, will not surmount his difficulties. Prayer will not pay debts, nor maintain credit, nor meet the emergencies of business. A man praying when he ought to be *working*, is brother in impiety to the man who is working when he ought to be praying. This concession cannot be too frankly made, nor too forcibly stated, by the ministers of the Gospel. It is not, however, in this way that the truly serious are in most danger of erring. When anything of this kind occurs, it is always in the case of men who never were consistent professors of religion; but doubtful characters from the first. Our error, in seasons of trial, is not in praying too much, but in praying too little, or less than usual. And this is a dangerous error, whatever be the cause or character of our trials. For its direct tendency is to turn " the mighty hand of God " against us, and thus to make all that is bad in our lot worse. Nothing, therefore, can be more unwise than a process which must grieve the Holy Spirit, and make God our enemy. Now this will be the effect of ceasing to pray, when the troubles of life are pressing. God both permits and sends these troubles for the express purpose of bringing us nearer to Himself, and for increasing the spirit and habit of prayer; and, therefore, if we allow our cares to break up our devotional habits, and thus to draw us away from God, we are sure to draw down upon ourselves His displeasure, in addition to all our other trials. And, when He takes up the rod to contend against us, who can tell how long or severely He may employ it! God does not, indeed, afflict willingly, nor grieve unnecessarily, the children of men; but He will not be neglected nor forgotten; He will not allow Himself to be deserted with impunity. God acts, invariably, with an express reference to our souls and eternity; and, therefore, unless He were to abandon them to a desolate eternity, He must multiply or prolong our troubles, if we allow them to estrange our hearts and habits from the throne of grace.

This is not the view we are apt to take of the matter. When we are injured by treachery, or wounded by unkindness ; when the badness of the times, or the baseness of false friends, wring our hearts, until we can think of nothing else ; we feel as if prayer, in this state of mind, would be mere mockery of God, and useless to ourselves. The loss, the injury, and the wounds of the heart, which we have sustained, are so present to our minds, and press so upon all our feelings, and keep up such an agitation of soul, that it seems impossible to pray. " What could we pray for at such a time, and in such a temper ?" In this way we reason. Or, if we do try to pray as usual, we soon find that we cannot. We are so haunted and harassed by the recollection of our grievances, that everything else is almost banished from our memory. We catch ourselves thinking of nothing else, even when our knees are bended, and our lips speaking before God. We find that, whilst going over our usual petitions in words, we have been going over, in thought, the whole history of our injuries. " And this," we justly say, " is not praying." We even conclude that it is better to keep out of our closet altogether for a time, than to enter into it with such feelings uppermost in our minds.

This is the view we are inclined to take of the matter. And, at first sight, it seems very plausible. It manifests, however, a sad lack of common sense, as well as of gracious principle, when we thus give way to such excuses. For what good can all our pondering upon our losses or crosses do ?   It will not repair the one or remove the other.   We are, in fact, *doubling* our cares every time we go over the history of them. Whilst thus placing them in every light, we are aggravating them.   Whilst dwelling upon them, we are embittering our remaining comforts, and actually risking the loss of everything ; for we may fret ourselves into a fever or frenzy, and thus be unfitted for all the duties and enjoyments of life.

It is upon this principle, as well as upon higher considerations, that God forbids all undue care.   It cannot be indulged with safety to our health of body or mind, nor with benefit to any of our interests.   Its direct tendency is to make all that is bad worse, and to embitter all that is sweet in our lot.   Accordingly, we have never mended anything that was wrong by vexing ourselves about it.   Whenever we have got over any grievance, it has been by an effort to forget it, or by praying down the memory of it.   Peace and composure of mind have never been regained until we returned to our old devotional habits.   This return, however, does not usually take place, until we are actually *tired* of brooding and fretting over our cares. We indulge "our vexation of spirit," until it work itself out by its own violence, or is displaced by some more absorbing subject.   This, however, is not the scriptural way of getting over the vexation and grievances of life.   Leaving them to die a natural death is not Christian prudence.   Yielding to their distracting influence, until we are sick of it, is not creditable to our principles, nor to our common sense. They ought to be met at once by prayer, and to be put down by it. And this is not impossible, however difficult it may seem at first sight. There is, in fact, no case of trial in which prayer is not an effectual antidote against disquietude and corroding anxiety. "The peace of God" can and will keep both the "heart and mind" of those who cast all their care upon God, "by supplication and prayer, with thanksgiving." Nothing can resist the sweet influence of this devotional habit.

If we doubt the truth of this, there is some grand defects in our ideas of prayer itself, or in our manner of praying, in reference to cares and vexations. Prayer, under them, must be regulated by scriptural rules, if we would experience the benefit of it. Now, one of these rules is, that it must be "with thanksgiving." If, therefore, we go to the throne of grace only to deplore our losses, only to unbosom our cares, or only to make known our wants, we have no warrant whatever to expect support or peace unto them. Our "requests" must be mingled with "thanksgiving," if we would succeed in obtaining "grace to help in time of need." No wonder ! for even when our cares are heaviest, and our wants most pressing, we have much cause for gratitude. In general, the comforts which are left with us are more than those which are taken away, whether they be property, friends, or business. And even then what is left is nothing compared with what is lost, there is always something remains worthy of being gratefully acknowledged.

However prone, therefore, we may He to lose, in what is lost, the recollection and estimate of what is left, God does not forget what is spared to us, nor forego His claims upon our gratitude.   He will be acknowledged for what we have, as well as applied to for what we want.   Instead, therefore, of going to our closets only to pour out griefs before Him, we ought to go also for the express purpose of reviewing with wonder, and recording with gratitude, every spared comfort and continued mercy.   This is an essential part of the devotional process of throwing off undue carefulness ; and, accordingly, it is also an effectual part.

"But," it may be said, "who can engage in thanksgiving, when his heart is bleeding, by unkindness, or treachery, or bereavement ?"   Why, all whose hearts have any hope of salvation.   Is the hope of eternal life such a trifle as to be unworthy of, or unfit for, a song of praise, whenever any of the comforts of this life are taken away ?   What a poor hold of it we must have, if we can forget it in the day of calamity !   What a low estimate we have formed of it, if it can be insipid whenever we are put out of the way by temporal things !   I do not think lightly of cares or crosses, vexations or grievances—they are hard to bear ; but what are they, compared with the wrath and curse of God, or with the agonies of despair ?   Any lot, out of hell, demands and deserves our fervent gratitude ; and where the hope of heaven is left in the bosom, no earthly loss can excuse silence.   But, in general, how many other comforts are left with it! The friends who remain true to us are more than those who have betrayed us. Our losses have not left us destitute. Our bereavements have not made us homeless. If a few have wounded our hearts, more have tried to pour balm into them. Besides, God has never forsaken us. God has never hurt our feelings by unkindness. God has never betrayed our confidence. He has been faithful, watchful, and tender, throughout all his dealings with us. And shall the ingratitude or baseness of others turn us against Him? Shall we cease to praise the Father of our mercies, because a fellow-creature deserves blame? Shall we resent our injuries upon God, upon the Saviour, or upon the Holy Spirit, by neglecting them, because others have acted unjustly towards us. The bare idea is equally shocking and absurd.

You see, you begin to feel now, that if, after any harassing or unhinging event, the first thing we did was to retire into the presence of God, to consider, first, our untouched property, our untouched comforts, our untouched friends, and our untouched hopes, we could not be so overcome as we usually have been, nor so much put out of the way. The review of what is left would compel thanksgiving ; and praise would fit the mind for prayer. But if we go into the closet choking and chafed with the sense of injury, and looking only at the persons who inflicted it, it is impossible to pray at all. Our breast must be cleared by *praise*, before it can be calmed by prayer, at such times.

This, however, is not the only thing necessary, in order to secure peace of mind under the trials of life. It is not every kind of praying that will meet our case. Even earnest supplication for pity and support is not fully to the point, when the heart is full of anger or vexation. Indeed, in that state, it cannot be comforted, and will not be humoured; for God will not countenance a bad spirit in his children. He may not always "rebuke" a wrong spirit in them; but he will only soothe them by *subduing* it. And he will teach you, as he did Jonah, to cease from saying, "I do well to be angry." Such being his rule in vouchsafing support and consolation to sufferers, it is self-evident that our prayers under the trials of life should include—

FIRST, *A distinct and humble acknowledgment of God's supreme right to permit these trials.* Until this be confessed, it is impossible to pray with pleasure or advantage. Indeed, we are not *suppliants*, at all, but *claimants*, whilst we consider it unjust or unkind, on the part of God, to permit these trials. As they come from the hand of man, they may be flagrantly unjust; but, as they come from the hand of God, they cannot be even unkind or unnecessary. They may be wholly undeserved by us, so far as man is concerned; but they are wholly deserved from God. He might justly permit and appoint far more and heavier trials than any we have ever experienced; for, whatever they be, "he hath not dealt with us according to our sins, nor rewarded us according to our iniquities." We do not understand the evil of sin, nor the necessity of holiness, if we deny or doubt this. The *punishment* of sin is wrath to the uttermost ; and, therefore, *chastisement* for sin, however severe, is, in fact, mercy.

It is by forgetting or overlooking this scriptural view of our trials, that they so fill us with care, and unfit us for devotion. We confine our attention to them as unmerited injuries from the hand of man, instead of regarding them also as merited chastisements from the hand of God. Accordingly, we cannot pray whilst we take this partial view of them. But we can pray, even when they press heaviest, if we are prepared to confess that we *deserve* them all, and more, from God. This confession is itself the best kind of prayer in times of trial. In fact, no other kind of prayer will be of any use, until we fully acknowledge before God that his judgments are just. Whoever, therefore, would regain peace of mind, or get over the unhappy and unholy feelings created by cares and vexations, must make up his mind to go fully into the duty of confession, however painful or mortifying it may seem to him at first. It will amply repay him ! He will feel himself a *new* man, from the moment he has humbly bowed to the sentence of God. The act of humiliation will pluck from his bosom the canker of pride, and thus make room again for the peace of God.

SECONDLY, *Our prayers under the trials of life, must include a distinct acknowledgment of the wisdom and kindness of God.* It is both wise and kind, as well as just, on the part of God, to try the faith and patience of believers. For how else could we fully ascertain the sincerity of our faith or love? We often doubt it, and pray that God would put it beyond all doubt. Now, the ordinary trials of life are the best tests of our sincerity : far better than extraordinary calamities are. Under heavy calamities we *must* submit, because we cannot resist. They also break down or soften the spirits, so that it is difficult to decide whether our feelings, under them, are from the weakness of nature, or the strength of grace. Whereas, the trials which leave us in full possession of all our faculties, and with some opportunities of surmounting them, prove what our principles are, and can bear. When, therefore, we do not, and dare not, quit the narrow way, even when it is thorny and rugged, our sincerity is demonstrated to ourselves and others. And it is delightful to feel that, though disconcerted and somewhat discouraged, the Saviour is dearer to us than anything we have lost. Then the soul gets a clear sight of its own principles, as John did when he said, "This is the victory which overcometh the world, even our faith." Now, if it be wise to bring us thus fully to the point, it must be kind to employ means which do it effectually. In praying, therefore, under them, this must be acknowledged before God. And the way to bring out the acknowledgment is to press home upon ourselves the questions—Which is better, to be uncertain of the reality of my faith, or to be sure of it ? To know that my heart is right with God, or to be in perpetual doubt of it ? To feel sure that I am won to the cross by the worth of salvation, and not bribed to it by the comforts of life ? Such questions search the heart and the reins. They throw us upon the *meaning* of our professions of faith and love. We have often said with Paul, " Yea, doubtless, I count all things but loss that I may be found in Christ ;" and this is easily said, when we are *losing* nothing. Accordingly, it is doubtful, not "doubtless," in our case, until we have " suffered the loss " of something, without shrinking from Christ. Paul had suffered the loss of " all things," when he avowed his adherence to the Saviour ; and, therefore, all things in his lot, and conduct, and temper, echoed back his " *doubtless !* "

To pray in the spirit thus characterised and commended, is not, indeed, easy. It is almost impossible at first, or by a direct effort. Such submission and gratitude, under vexing and wasting cares, can only be acquired by concentrating our prayers for a time upon our *eternal* interests. They must be all in all before our temporal interests can be seen in their true light. The temporal will seem unduly important, until the eternal appear as they are—infinitely important ! No one can calmly lose this world's goods, or keep a loose hold of them, who has not a firm hold upon the glories of the world to come. His efforts to reason down, or pray down, disquietude, will defeat themselves, until he " can read," or determines to read

> " His title clear,
> To mansions in the skies."

It was only when Paul looked at the things which were unseen and eternal, that he was able to counterbalance the weight of the things which were seen and temporal. And this maxim is as necessary in our case, however much less than his our trials may be.

Are you then safe for eternity? Are you *sure* of your personal interest in Christ and heaven? If not, let all your thoughts and prayers centre upon the settlement, the immediate and perfect settlement, of this chief point. This process will soon place temporal things before you as they appear to a *dying* man. It is not by an effort that he forgets them, but by the influence of an opening eternity. Dwell, therefore, on the sides of eternity, with the question, " Am I safe?" until you can answer it before God and man, on scriptural grounds. Thus prayer will produce peace, even in your case.*

* *See* " ETERNITY REALIZED: or, a Guide to the Thoughtful ;" the third volume of the Author's Guides.

CHAPTER X.

THE SAVIOUR'S DEVOTIONAL SPIRIT.

"JESUS went up into a mountain:" for what purpose? To view the Judean landscape, while the setting sun was flushing the lake of Gennesaret, and tinging with golden radiance the adjacent wilderness? No.

"When the evening was come, Jesus was there *alone.*" Why?—That He might watch the rising of the evening star, and mark the lamps of heaven kindling in clusters and constellations throughout the hemisphere? No. Did He, then, ascend the mountain to enjoy repose? The Saviour needed rest at the time, for He had spent the day in healing the sick, and feeding the hungry, under a scorching sun, and amidst a crowding multitude. But it was not for *rest* that He retired: He "went up to a mountain apart to *pray.*" Was this devotional exercise less sublime than gazing on the gilded landscape and the glowing firmament? Those who ascend mountains, voluntarily and alone, do so, in general, to indulge poetic or scientific taste ; to command the prospect, and to commune with nature in silence and solitude. Jesus ascended to pray ; and by prayer, to commune with God : a nobler communion than poets or philosophers ever had with nature, in her majestic or lovely scenes. And yet how few are alive to the sublimity of devotional solitude ! Praying in secret to the Father who seeth in secret, is an exercise equally solemn and august ; but how little interest it excites to say of a man, *he is alone praying !*

Tell men of taste, that their favourite poet is *alone* amidst the scenery of the lakes or the Grampians ; alone on the Alps or the Andes ; alone in the Coliseum of Rome, or amidst the Pyramids of Egypt ; and immediately his admirers will realise his emotions, and dwell with him, in spirit, amidst clouds and cataracts, rocks and ruins, and feel as if he were more than mortal. But tell them that he is alone praying ; and that moment the charm will be dissolved, and the man pitied as insane, or despised as fanatical. So lightly is devotional solitude esteemed !

Tell scientific men, that the first astronomer of the age is alone in the chief observatory in the world, with the most powerful telescopes ever lifted to the heavens ; and all kindred minds will at once kindle in prospect of his discoveries. The silence and solitude of his post are held sublime, and felt to be in harmony with the silent sweep of the celestial orbs, and the music of the spheres. But tell his admirers, that he often pauses, amidst the roll and radiance of the heavenly bodies, to pray; and although one of their own poets has said that

> " An undevout astronomer is mad,"

his devotion will be esteemed madness or weakness.

> " The poet's eye, in a fine frenzy rolling,
> Doth glance from heaven to earth, from earth to heaven,"

and is almost adored; but the penitent's eyes, swimming in tears of contrition, and hardly daring to look up, even when *alone* before God, are despised by the generality of mankind. But "a broken and a contrite heart, O God, Thou wilt not despise." The astronomer tracing the stars in their courses, and tracking the devious comet in its flight, is held to be a star of the first magnitude in the mental system—strong in understanding, and lofty in genius. But the Christian, retired to pray, is held to be almost mean-spirited. And yet—he lifts his adoring eyes to heaven, of which the incarnate " brightness of the Father's glory" is both " the morning star" and " the sun of righteousness;" and in His light sees the landscape of eternity illuminated—the valley of the shadow of death irradiated with the Divine presence, and all the intermediate track of time basking under the eye of Providence. Often, when alone praying, he finds his closet the very gate of heaven, and feels as if " open vision" would follow his intimate communion with God and the Lamb. Whatever, therefore, may be thought or said, by taste, science, or ignorance, of going apart, and being alone to pray, devotional solitude is often exhilarating, and always soothing.

It is commended by the high example, and commanded by the high authority, of the Saviour—

> " Cold mountains and the midnight air,
>   Witnessed the fervour of His prayer. "

His example does not, of course, enforce an ascent to a mountain, in order to pray. He went up into a mountain from necessity—not from choice; because, as the Son of man, He had not where to lay His head; no home or closet. To those who have both, His command is—" Enter into thy closet." And we learn, from His example, that *inconvenience* must not prevent secret prayer. Here was the Saviour upon a lonely mountain—exposed to the cold winds and dews of the night—the ground damp beneath His knees, and the air chill around Him ; and yet He prayed —prayed long; the morning star often finding Him where the evening star had left Him. We have not such inconveniences to surmount. What is a cold room in winter, or a close room in summer, compared to the hoary side of a bleak and dreary mountain at midnight? And yet, how often are cold and heat allowed to hinder or hurry over secret prayer ! Let sloth look to the Saviour's retirement, and blush ! God might have enjoined us to ascend such a mountain whenever we prayed ; and if He had commanded it, the duty would have been indispensable ; but, in tender accommodation to our comfort, He has granted us, what He withheld from His incarnate Son—a house; and says, " Enter into thy closet."

The Saviour's example proves that the *fatigue* of labour must not prevent secret prayer. He had spent the day until the evening in active exertion amongst the multitude that followed Him into the wilderness. During all the time He had been under a burning sun in a sandy desert, and had afterwards to ascend the mountain alone. And there—neither shelter nor refreshment awaited Him; but, although thus exhausted and exposed, He closed the labours of the day by prayer. Now, His example ought to have all the authority of a law—all the influence of a charm upon His disciples. We do not come home more fatigued than He was. He had no house—no domestic comforts—neither shelter nor pillow for His sacred head ; and yet He went apart to pray. He will remind the prayerless of this fact.

The Saviour's example proves that even deeds ot *charity*, and great exertions for the poor and afflicted, must not set aside secret prayer. He closed a day of mighty effort on behalf of suffering humanity, by going apart to pray. And surely if serving others must not prevent devotional solitude, serving ourselves must not be allowed to do so : if acts of charity will not excuse neglect, the labours of industry cannot : if giving money to the poor be no plea for the omission of prayer, making money is not a valid one. Accordingly, while " diligence in business " is expressly enjoined, " fervency of spirit " in prayer rests upon the same high and unalterable authority. Pray or perish, is the alternative set before us in the Gospel.

The Saviour's example proves that no *strength* of character or of grace can render devotional solitude unnecessary. He who had the Spirit without measure —who knew no sin—who was full of grace, and in whom Satan could find nothing to work upon—He went apart to pray. He held neither the fulness of His Godhead, nor the perfection of His humanity, as a reason for restraining prayer. And surely nothing that we have " attained " can render us independent of secret devotion ! " The servant is not greater than his Lord." If, therefore, Satan, or sloth, or pride, say, we may do with less prayer than at first, let us hear the insinuation as we should the assertion, that we can do with less glorying in the Cross than we began with.

But here an important question forces itself upon the mind—Why did the Saviour pray? He did pray often and fervently ; and the fact has been perverted into an argument against His proper divinity. But remember what He prayed for : it was chiefly for *others :* and when it was for Himself, never for ability to *save*—never for virtue to give efficacy to His *atonement*—never for strength to redeem. No—all His petitions in His own behalf were for the helps required by His human nature. He could, indeed, have drawn on the resources of His own personal Godhead ; but it was necessary that the co-operation of the Father in the work of redemption should appear ; and, therefore, all the dependence of His humanity was thrown on the Father's goodwill: and thus prayer was rendered both necessary and proper. Besides, secret devotion is more than prayer: it is also *communion* with God. Now, what is more natural, and consistent, and becoming, than that the Son should retire to commune with the Father? For, having dwelt in His bosom from eternity, it might be expected that He would maintain the ordinary intimacy, both for its own sake, and that it might be known that neither distance nor incarnation had interrupted their fellowship. Instead, therefore, of derogating from His divinity, such prayer harmonises with the highest ideas of Godhead—being in fact a specimen of its devout communion. Besides, in praying, as in all practical duty, the Saviour was acting as the *example* of His followers. He had taught His disciples to pray; and He illustrated and enforced the lesson by His own devotional habits: and if it was worthy of His divinity to inculcate devotion, it could not be unworthy of Him to *exemplify* it. "When He putteth forth His own sheep, He goeth before them:" He sent them into secret to pray, and He Himself went apart to pray.

The Saviour consulted our interest as well as His Father's glory when He enjoined devotional solitude upon His disciples; for, in the *best* frame of mind, a Christian requires to be alone at times. The privacy of the domestic altar is not sufficiently "apart," when the heart is full and overflowing with adoring and melting views of sovereign and free grace. The full-souled exclamation, "Why me, Lord!" with its tones and tears, is fit only for the ear of God. And when the witness of the Spirit is strong, and the seal of the Spirit bright—when the soul is borne away amongst "the deep things of God," and the dazzling scenes of eternity—we must be alone, or lose one half of the enjoyment. Even a family, however endeared, would be a check, at these sacred moments, on the full flow of devotional feeling, and on the flush of a hope full of immortality. Solitude is the real element of these raptures. But then—the Christian is not alone : the mount of communion is covered with "horses of fire, and chariots of fire." He is alone—"with an innumerable company of angels, and with the spirits of just men made perfect."

Solitude is also peculiarly suitable to the *worst* frames of a Christian's mind. The tones and terms in which backsliding, or indeed any sin, can be deplored in the domestic or social circle, are both too general and tame for the emotions of a contrite spirit. David was alone when he said, "I have gone astray like a lost sheep." Asaph was alone when he said, "I was as a beast before Thee." Ephraim was alone when he smote upon his thigh, and acknowledged that he had been as "a bullock unaccustomed to the yoke." And our secret sorrows and shame are not fit even for the ear of our families. They might be misunderstood and misinterpreted by others ; whereas, He who heareth in secret can heal in secret. And what a sanctuary is solitude for the expression of all those feelings which, even at home, can only be breathed in general and gentle terms ! It will not do to utter before our families all our fears of death, nor all our anxieties for them. It will not do to unburden and unbosom all the heart to any one but God. God seeth and heareth in secret. What a mercy ! What a wise and kind arrangement ! "It is good for me to draw nigh unto God." alone !

CHAPTER XI.

COMMUNION WITH GOD IN AFFLICTION.

HILST it is still true that "through much tribulation we must enter into the kingdom of God," it is, happily, our lot to live at a time, and in a place, free from the fiery trial of persecution and martyrdom. Neither bonds nor imprisonments await us in the service of God. Our property is safe, and our good name hardly in danger. " Cruel mockings," for righteousness' sake, do not come from the *public* voice now ; and "scourgings," for the sake of Christ, would be denounced even by the enemies of the cross of Christ.

This happy change in the public mind and manners demands our grateful acknowledgment. For if we are at times staggered and almost overwhelmed by the ordinary trials of life, what would be the effect of such fiery trials as the first Christians had to endure? If we call, and feel our heaviest troubles to be, a *furnace*, what should we have thought of the Babylonian furnace, and the flames of martyrdom? If we shrink from a sneer or sarcasm, now that it is no longer backed by the sword, how should we have acted when it was the signal for guards to arrest, or for the rabble to stone Christians?

These are not the trials of our times. It was, however, to such trials, chiefly, that the greatest of the " great and precious promises" refer. It is not exactly of chronic nor acute diseases of the body that the Saviour and the apostles speak, when they comfort the Church under her manifold afflictions. It was not over sick-beds by name, nor over mere death-beds by name, that they opened the visions of all-sufficient grace, and of an eternal weight of glory, but over racks, and scaffolds, and dungeons.

These facts are startling at first sight! They are, however, facts ; and, therefore, should neither be concealed nor overlooked. We, indeed, have formed the habit of applying any promise of grace or strength to any trial whatever. We do not hesitate to draw as freely upon the "strong consolation" of the well-ordered covenant, when in sickness or pain, as the martyrs did when they were imprisoned and impaled. With not a tithe of their sufferings, we lay claim to all their supports—so far as these were derived from the promises.

Now, it is not to dispute the propriety of this conduct that I place it in this light. It is highly proper that all suffering Christians, whatever be the kind or degree of their trials, should take to themselves all the consolation which is to be found in the word of God.

It is, however, equally proper that they should clearly understand their warrant and welcome to do so. For, it is not right *because they do so;* but because God *allows* it to be done. It will, therefore, be best done by those who understand the Divine warrant for comforting themselves with the great and precious promises.

Look, then, at the facts of the case. These promises were made, in the first instance, to Christians whose lives, property, and reputation were in constant peril because of their adherence to Christ. And yet these very promises you apply in your own case, under the natural diseases and decay of the body; under the losses and crosses incident to the ordinary business of life ; under the vexations and sorrows inseparable from all human affairs. Now, where and what is your warrant for this appropriation of comforts, which belonged originally to sufferers who were " a spectacle to the world and to angels?" What right have you to draw from the sacred fountains which were open to refresh martyrs and confessors? Is it the lunacy of self-love that has betrayed you into a false estimate of your own importance? Or, is it the love of God that has made "all the promises *yea and amen*, in Christ Jesus," to all who love the Lord Jesus in sincerity, whatever be the kind or the degree of their afflictions?

This is the fact. Accordingly, there is not one well-ordered covenant for slight sufferers, and another better-ordered covenant for great sufferers ; but one

" ordered in all things and sure," for both alike.   For, however the Spirit of God may have applied these strong consolations more sensibly and fully to the hearts of the martyrs than He does now to our hearts, it was these consolations that He did apply.   As it is the same pole-star in calm and in storm, on a wreck and in a new ship, that the seaman steers his course by—so it is the same light which shines from the promises upon all the afflicted children of God, whatever be the difference of their afflictions.   " Were it not so, I would have told you," is an expression of the Saviour's, which may well and safely be applied here. Indeed, " were it not so," another covenant or an alteration of " the new covenant," would and must have been introduced when persecution was withdrawn.   But the consolations were not changed when the sufferings were changed.   The scaffolds are fallen, but the covenant standeth fast : the sword is sheathed, but the balm of Gilead is undiminished ; the flames are quenched, but the prospects of future glory remain undiminished.   These assertions require to be proved by facts, and confirmed by reasons.   Now, it is the fact—

1. That believers sustain the same relation to God that the martyrs did.   Christians did not cease to be the sons and daughters of the Lord God Almighty, when they ceased to be the victims of persecution. Adoption remains the same under our " vine and fig-tree," where none dare to make us afraid, as under the cross, the stake, or the axe of martyrdom.   All who

love the Saviour are as much the children of God as the noble army of martyrs.

This is true even when we are not suffering under the mighty hand of God ; and surely it does not become untrue when we are under the rod. Chastisement is itself a proof of sonship. "If ye endure chastisement," says Paul, " God dealeth with you as with sons."

Here, then, is the first ground which you should take in order to communion with God, when His fatherly hand presses heavily upon your spirits. Its pressure does not disprove your sonship. Even its long continuance does not render your adoption doubtful. God does not cast off when He casts down. For wise and gracious purposes He impoverishes many of the children, and chastises them all ; but He never *disinherits* any of them. They may think, and even say, in the day of calamity, "Surely, God would not put such a bitter cup into my hand, if I were a child of His ; surely He would not contend so long and sharply if He had put me amongst His children !" But all this is a mistake. The argument should run just the other way. The reverse is the truth, however difficult it may be to believe so at first. It is difficult, I readily grant. But look again, and more fully, at your own case. Before this heavy trial came upon you, you ventured to hope that you were a child of God. Why ? Your freedom from this affliction was no proof nor mark of sonship. Neither the ease, nor the comfort of your former circumstances, gave you any right or reason for cherishing the hope of adoption. Accordingly, you did not think then that they did. Remember, any hope you ventured to take up then was founded entirely upon the work of Christ and the word of God. And had any one asserted or insinuated, at that time, that you were grounding the hope of sonship upon your *temporal* circumstances, you would have disclaimed, with warmth, the unworthy imputation, and affirmed that Christ was " all in all" in your hope. Well, if *easy* circumstances had, thus, nothing to do with the Spirit of adoption when you began to enjoy it —what have *trying* circumstances to do with it? It does not belong to prosperity, as such ; nor to adversity, as such. It is the fruit of faith in the atonement ; and the atonement is not altered in its essence or aspect, however the aspect of Providence may be changed. All your real ground for considering God as your Father, and for pouring out your heart to Him, remains, therefore, the same as ever. Or, if there be any alteration in it, it is for the *better;* for you are warranted to put an interpretation upon your adversity, which prosperity will not often bear. The trials of believers are declared by God to be proofs of sonship ; but their worldly prosperity is never explained in this way. It is the fact—

2. That the present sufferings of believers are sent for the same moral purpose as the persecution of the martyrs was permitted—by God. Now, as far as that moral purpose terminated in themselves, it was, that " they might be partakers of His holiness," and thus

conformed to the image of His Son. And as this is the grand and final purpose of God in the case of all His children, He has left open to them all the same "wells of salvation" that He laid open to the first believers. It is, therefore, because God is pursuing the same end, now as then, that He continues to us all the original motives to holiness. It was endeared to martyrs and confessors by the hope of eternal life —by the promise of sufficient grace—by the witness of the Spirit—and by the special presence of God. Without these, even *their* trials would not have produced true holiness. Neither racks nor flames would have purified their hearts, apart from the consolations of the Gospel.

It is not, therefore, entirely wonderful, that all the promises remain, and hold equally good, in our case. They are wanted—they are indispensably necessary, if we are to be made partakers of the Divine holiness. Nothing else, and nothing less, than the "good hope through grace," granted to the first believers, is sufficient to sanctify present or future believers. For sanctification is not the effect of affliction, any further than affliction sends us to the Word and Spirit of God. Indeed, affliction itself requires to be sanctified; for its natural influence, and inevitable consequence, when unaccompanied by the mighty working of the eternal Spirit, are to harden the heart. "Why should ye be stricken any more?" said Isaiah, to the Jewish Church, when they had vexed and grieved the Holy Spirit: "ye will only rebel more and more."

Here, then, is another ground upon which communion with God may be renewed in your case. And it is as solid as holiness is essential. Now, you know and believe that, without holiness, no man shall see the Lord. And you *feel* that the strokes of His Providence are destroying both the power and the love of sin. You may be unhinged, and agitated, and almost overwhelmed, by your trials ; but they are not strengthening your besetting sin, nor lessening your hatred or fear of any sin. Whatever else be their effect upon you, they are not softening the aspect of evil, nor increasing your love to the world. The reverse is their effect. The world seems to you a poor portion for your immortal soul ; and all sin is more than ever hateful. And are *you* afraid to pray? Do *you* doubt the paternal aspect of your chastisement? What! holiness advancing—and you doubting your *sonship?* Sin abhorrent—and you unchristianising yourself? Why, if anything be certain, it is that a soul dying to the world and sin is *alive* unto God. "In this the children of God are manifest."

Consider! The salutary effect of your trials, in thus setting your heart against all that is hateful to God, proves far more in *favour* of your interest in the love of God, than your trials prove against it. You say that you cannot reconcile them with an interest in the *love* of God. I say that you cannot reconcile their holy influence with any suspicion of the *hatred* of God. But what is my opinion on the subject? God Himself says, that "whom He loveth He chasteneth,

and scourgeth every son whom He receiveth." Mark,
He does not say that whom He loveth, He prospereth
in the world, but whom He chasteneth. If, then,
your afflictions are producing the same holy effects as
those promoted in the martyrs, by "great tribulation,"
you are as much warranted, as they were, to regard
God as your God for ever and ever, and to calculate
upon Him being your guide until death.

Now, it is by believing this that you must regain
your composure and freedom in prayer. You cannot
regain them in any other way. For when the spirit
of prayer is lost, under the mysterious dispensations
of Providence, it can only be recovered by turning to
the mystery of grace. And, according to that, things
are never wrong, nor going wrong, with the soul, when
the work of *sanctification* is going on. Now, it is not
going back, because you are less composed, and more
shaken than usual. Composure is, indeed, a good
thing in its proper place, and a good sign under certain circumstances :—but there is something better,
both as a sensation and a sign ; and that is, a heart
agitated and agonised by a sense of the evil of sin.
For many things may produce a tranquil mind ;
whereas it is only the Spirit of God that can create
loathing and detestation against sin. Whoever, therefore, feels this, need not be afraid to commune with
God as his own Father. Indeed, this itself is communion, or fellowship, in the very feelings which are
the glory of His character—His love of holiness, and
His hatred of sin It is also the fact—

3. That nothing less than the hope of the glory which is to be revealed, can reconcile or soothe the mind, even under the present trials of life and godliness. A hope full of immortality is as much wanted in a sick chamber, as it was in a Roman prison ; in poverty, as in spoliation ; in the loss of relations by death, as in their loss by martyrdom. Perhaps more so, in one sense ; for, in solitary or obscure affliction, there is no appeal made to our passions or senses ; whereas martyrdom, by its publicity and splendour, was calculated to inspire no small share of the fortitude it called for. But, however this may be, one thing is certain,—that afflictions have not a sanctifying influence, nor are they well sustained, where there is not a well-founded hope of heaven. However strange it may be, therefore, in theory, that our inferior sufferings should have, or require, all the great and precious promises which were made to the first Christians, it is only the sober fact—that we do require them all, in order to possess our souls in patience. The prospect of heaven is not too bright, nor the consolation that is in Christ too strong, even in the day of *our* calamity. Whatever, therefore, might be theoretically argued, to prove that less ought to suffice now that there is far less to suffer, the fact is, that less does not suffice. All experience demonstrates that there is neither true holiness nor happiness under calamity, but where there is a good hope, through grace, of an eternal weight of glory. Now, this is the hope which must inspire and sustain

communion with God in the furnace. This hope must be in the midst of every furnace of affliction, as the Son of God was in the Babylonian furnace, if, like the three Hebrews, we would be free or unhurt. Our own reasonings against impatience, and the remonstrances of others against it, will not prevent nor suppress impatience. It has but one effectual antidote —the hope of eternal life. The prospect of better days and better things in this life, is not, indeed, without its influence ; but it is not in praying for them that the soul gets into communion with God. It is in praying for meetness for the inheritance of the saints in light, that we obtain true and transporting fellowship with Him.

CHAPTER XII.

SACRAMENTAL COMMUNION WITH GOD AND THE LAMB.

IT is pleasing to remember how many, in all ages of the Christian Church, have celebrated the death of the Saviour, at the sacramental table. That has never, indeed, been a crowded table, where the guests have been required to wear the "wedding garment;" but neither has it ever been a forsaken table. Some were always as constant at the sacramental supper on earth, as they are now at "the marriage supper of the Lamb" in heaven. Many of them commemorated His death at the risk of their own lives. The mountain tops were not too cold, nor the caves of the wilderness too damp, nor the tombs at midnight too dreary, for the first Christians, when persecution drove them to *secret* sacraments. They loved their Lord, and therefore testified their attachment to Him at all hazards, and under all hardships.

Such were the primitive believers. The world then

thought them fools; but now even the world itself applauds their heroism, and remembers them more than it does the guests who sat at the banqueting tables of the Belshazzars and Cæsars of antiquity. It is pleasing to remember, also, that there are now sacramental tables in many nations, where there was only "the table of devils" then. When the first sacraments were celebrating in Judea and Greece, human sacrifices were prevalent and popular in Britain. Hallowed be the day, when the first Christian sacrament was administered in the lands of our fathers ! Its date is unknown; its place unmarked; its form uncertain; but its "sweet influences" have been incalculable. It was the "olive leaf" (whoever was the dove that brought it), which proved that the flood of Druidism was subsiding.

It is pleasing to remember, also, that even since we became communicants there are many sacramental tables, where there was only the table of devils when we were born. There is now one in China, a few in India, and many in Africa and the South Sea Islands. And still they are multiplying. They will become as general as the domestic table of families; until all on earth vie with all in heaven, in "showing the Lord's death until He come."

By thus remembering "the dead in Christ," and anticipating the unborn who shall be given to Christ, we forget in some measure, or rather get above, our *own* fears and trials. We thus feel ourselves to be a part of an immense army—the first companies of which are already crowned with victory, and the last sure to be more than conquerors, by the blood of the Lamb. This identification is as useful as it is sublime.

When a Christian thinks only of himself, and for himself, he is easily discouraged, and feels, at times, ready to sink. But when he realises himself as one of God's family, and as one of Christ's flock, and remembers how many are arrived at the kingdom in safety, and how many are with him in the wilderness —he sees and feels that he, too, may overcome. Whilst he looks only at himself, he can hardly conceive how everlasting wings should be over him, or how he should be welcome to take shelter under them. But when he pauses to observe how many they shelter, and how widely they are expanded, he is encouraged to creep under their shadow.

When he thinks only of himself, he can hardly see how the Saviour can take any lively or constant interest in him; nor how the Holy Spirit can bear with his infirmities; but when he pauses to consider, that the Great Shepherd's flock is too large to be forsaken by a good Shepherd, or by a Spirit who is "the Comforter," he feels that, although the weakest of the lambs of that flock, he may yet share in its Shepherd's tenderness, and venture into all its green pastures, and up to all its still waters, in company.

When he looks only at his own trials, he can hardly see how a special Providence should take up his case, or hold up his goings; but when he pauses to consider how many have been guarded and guided, and how many need as much guidance and guardianship as himself—they are both so many, that he feels, through all his soul, that the God of love is not likely to leave nor forsake them ; and thus he, too, ventures to cast all his care upon a wise and watchful Providence.

It is thus also that he is encouraged at times to venture to the Lord's table.   His own sense of unfitness and unworthiness would keep him away, did not others, who confess the same, continue to come.   Not that he gets over his fears by considering himself as good as others ; but he sees that the best of others have had similar fears, and that, if they had yielded to them, they could never have become such exemplary Christians.   He sees that there has been an intimate and inseparable connection between their growth in grace, and their adherence to the sacrament.   Nor can he overlook or forget the fact, that all that was bad has become worse, in the case of those who have given up sacraments.   And thus these examples bring him to the point : "I may become," he says, "an apostate, by keeping away ! I may be established, strengthened, and settled, by keeping the feast."

These are not, indeed, the highest motives for adhering to the sacramental table ; but they are legitimate and powerful motives.   So also is the consideration, that your absence may injure or pair others.   For, by not communing with your brethren you may prevent or mar their communion with God Some of them are sure to miss you, and almost as sure to be affected by it. Those, especially, who encouraged and welcomed you to the sacrament, and those also whom you may have encouraged and welcomed to it, cannot but wonder at your absence. They ought, indeed, to be better employed, than in thinking of an absent friend. The "remembrance" of the Saviour ought to engross and absorb their whole soul. You feel and confess this. Do not, then, divide or divert their hearts from Him, by deserting them. Remember, how you would have felt, had you missed them, when you *began* to communicate! And as their presence has often encouraged you, let your presence encourage them.

There is more connection between this tender regard to the feelings of others, and communion with God, than seems generally understood. Many appear to imagine, that it is of little consequence how they feel towards their brethren at the sacrament, if they are not at open variance with them. That, it is generally acknowledged, is incompatible with communion with God. And, whether acknowledged or not, it is found to be so, both by offenders and the offended. Neither find much comfort or benefit at the Lord's table, whilst breaches or heartburnings are unhealed. This loss of enjoyment, is not, however, confined to alienated brethren. It is sustained by *indifferent* brethren also; and in a degree that ought to startle them, even if they are unconscious of any studied indifference. For the sacrament is as much intended to promote the fellowship of the members with each other, as the fellowship of the body with the Head. Indeed, the *unbroken* bread is as truly and intentionally an emblem of a united Church, as the broken bread is of the crucified Saviour. It is not enough, therefore, to remember the Saviour when we approach His table. He, of course, should be the supreme object of our attention ; but not to the exclusion of His people. A kind look or thought towards them will not displease Him, nor distract us. He is not *jealous* of brotherly love.

We mistake sadly, when we imagine that we cannot afford to think at all of the Church, whilst we are at the sacrament. It is quite true, that we have each so much to think of in our own case, that it *seems* more than enough at that time. Our own hearts are so unmanageable, that any concern for others appears both impossible and out of place, when we are trying to commune with the Saviour for ourselves. But, what if a momentary identification of ourselves with our brethren should be the best way of getting into communion with the Saviour Himself?—what if He who is "not ashamed to call them his brethren," hide His face from us, until we from the heart acknowledge them as our brethren ? This is not unlikely. Paul evidently held it to be certain, that, apart from being "rooted and grounded" in mutual love, believers could not "comprehend the heights, and depths, and lengths, and breadths, of the love of Christ." Now these are

"The sweet wonders of the cross,"

that we desire to comprehend at the sacrament. But, apart from cherishing unfeigned love to the brethren, we are not warranted to expect any enrapturing or realising manifestation of them. For, do remember, it is as much in connection with loving one another, as with loving Himself, that the Saviour promises to "manifest" Himself to His disciples.

This is the law of the house. And it is as reasonable as it is authoritative. You may have overlooked it hitherto, or not weighed it duly. But it is intimately connected with all the enjoyment which the sacrament is intended to promote. And if you have wondered and wept, because you have often missed enjoyment at the sacrament, it is high time for you to search out the secret causes of your disappointment.

Now, whatever other causes may have led to the loss of sacramental enjoyment, the want of a really "right spirit" towards your brethren is one cause of it. You may not, indeed, have behaved ill, nor carried yourself haughtily, towards any of them. No one may have any just reason to complain of your conduct or spirit as a communicant. You may be able even to appeal to all the Church, and to the omniscience of its Head, that you injure no one and despise no one. But, whilst all this is very creditable to you, and more than many can say for themselves, it is not all that devolves on you, even if you can add to it, that you never refuse to help the poor of the flock. All this may be done without "charity" (1 Cor. xiii. 3). The real question to meet is, Do you love the brethren, for the truth's sake which dwelleth in them, and because they are your brethren in Christ? This is the grand apostolic reason for mutual love in the Church. But if you love only a few, who happen to please you, and them, chiefly for what they are to you, rather than for what they are to Christ, you overlook this reason, and make yourself the centre of your affections. You may not intend to do this; but it comes to this, if you care little or nothing about those who are not your personal friends. You ought, indeed, to love them who love you; but you are equally bound to love all who love the Saviour.

It will not do, in answer to this, to say, that you stand in doubt of some of your fellow-members. That may be your own fault, in regard to some of them. They may be as worthy as yourself, if you knew them as well. And, in the case of those who are justly doubted, it is your duty to be faithful to them. If you know to a certainty, that any nominal brother is an immoral man, you are as much bound to reprove him, and to bring the matter to an issue, as he is bound to reform.

It is not necessary, however, to go into extreme cases. It is not from them that the neglect of brotherly love springs chiefly; but from our own inattention to the law of that love. Now, it is exceeding broad! It embraces all the personal friends of the Saviour, just because they are His friends. You are bound to love them, because He has loved them, even as He has loved us; and because they love Him as sincerely as we do. Accordingly, we should feel and admit the force of this claim at once, were we to sit down at an African or an Indian sacramental table. There, it would be impossible to look round upon a circle of brethren without a glow of brotherly love. Our hearts would thrill at the sight of so many brands plucked from the burning. We could not suppress our love to them, were we to try the experiment. We could not, by any effort, go into cold and jealous calculations of their comparative wealth or worth. All such considerations would be swallowed up in the high consciousness that we were associated with the friends of Jesus.

And are His friends less valuable at home? Is there less of His love displayed in a Church of British, than in a Church of African, converts? Why, then, do not we take an equal interest in the former?

The cases are not, indeed, parallel, in all respects. An African Church is a novelty; whereas a British Church is almost a matter of course; and we are too much the creatures of circumstances, to be as much affected by what is common as by what is uncommon. I readily grant, therefore, that the appeal to our senses is not the same at home that it would be abroad. Any group of Africans or Indians would, however engaged, arrest our attention, and interest our feelings, more than the same number of our own countrymen, similarly engaged. Africans themselves would be less affected by the sight of a British Church than we should by the sight of an African church;—because they must, of course, regard it as only what might be expected in Britain.

These concessions and distinctions ought to be made. But, after making them, thus fully and freely, there is still enough in the case, both to warrant and point an argument, on behalf of brotherly love at the sacrament. For, the utmost that can be said of any Church, in heathen lands, is, that " Christ loved them, and gave Himself for them." Their calling and election cannot be carried higher than to the purpose of God ; nor their redemption higher than to the blood of the Lamb ; nor their conversion higher than to the power of the Holy Spirit ; and to this height, the salvation of all may be equally traced. There is therefore, a defect in our spiritual discernment, whenever we can look upon real converts without real pleasure. For we should be delighted to meet the lowest of them in heaven ! There, we shall never think of what was their rank on earth. It will be enough to secure our love, there, that they were loved by our Father, and ransomed by our Saviour, and sanctified by our Comforter. Every believer we meet around the throne will be hailed and held as a "brother," because he is a "companion" in the New Song of the cross. Why, then, should it not be so on earth ?

These are not the considerations which you expected to be most prominent, in an essay on sacramental communion with God and the Lamb. You most likely, began to read it in the hope that you might find some touching hints, which would warm or melt your heart; and thus enable you to "go unto the altar of God," with more joy or composure than you could command when you were there last. Are you, then, disappointed? You ought not to be so. You have, indeed, a right to expect that a minister, enforcing and commending the sacrament, should also bring before you a full-orbed view of the great Sacrifice which it commemorates. For that, being the chief thing, ought to have the chief place. Well, just because it is the chief thing in the sacrament, I am intent on placing you in that spirit and position towards it, which are most in accordance with it. Now, that accordant position is identification with all who are "heirs together" with you, "of the grace of life;" and that accordant spirit is, love to them as joint heirs of eternal life.

It is also of great importance to bear in mind that *mournful* sacraments are not useless. We are apt to regard these sad solemnities as sad disappointments; and, if we miss enjoyment, to imagine that we have communicated in vain. But this is a mistake.

Neither God nor the Lamb is dishonoured or displeased, nor are we unprofited, when sacraments do nothing but *humble* us. We have not come to the Altar in vain, when we retire from it wondering that our blood was not mingled with our sacrifices. Nothing is useless that compels us to lay our "mouth in the dust, if so be there may be hope." And this is the effect of our sad sacraments. They lay us in the very dust of self-abasement. And, what is not less valuable, they make us feel, through all our soul, that we need more than ever to be watchful. For now that we cannot wring from our hearts one warm emotion, nor command one holy feeling, how easily temptations might overcome, or trials overwhelm us! The solemn questions—"Where will all this end?" "What has brought on this utter loss of first love?" —reveal, as they flash across our darkened spirit, dangers which make us tremble both at and for ourselves. Now, although such dread discoveries, like afflictions, are not joyous, but grievous; "nevertheless, afterward," they yield the peaceable fruit of righteousness unto them who are exercised by them.

When, however, there is a succession of sad or dull sacraments; and when communicants, month after month, retire from the altar of God weeping or trembling; and where the desolation of soul cannot be traced to the indulgence of any bad habit or temper, there must, in such a case, be some misapprehension of the Gospel. Now, the most prevalent mistake is, that faith can work *empty-handed;* or that the principle of it can work by love, even when it is not exercised in believing the promises of the God of love. Faith is, indeed, a principle, and a vital one; but (like the bee's power of making honey, which is of no use apart from the nectar of flowers), it cannot work by love without believing the motives to love. The bee cannot make honey from water, nor yet from the dew of the morning; no more can faith extract comfort or

hope from threatenings, or produce joy by dwelling on
the dark side of things. We might just as well, and
more wisely, expect that our power of seeing should
cheer us apart from *looking*, or our power of hearing
apart from *listening*, as expect that faith can comfort
us apart from believing " comfortable words." Why
are we so prone to drop all our *common sense*, when
we try to exercise or examine our faith? Whenever
we want to be cheered by the power of seeing, we
look abroad on the landscape of nature, or on the
achievements of art, and dwell on their beauties and
sublimities until the eye affects the heart. We never
gaze on vacancy, nor on deformity, when we wish to
be delighted. In like manner, when we are intent on
being cheered by the exercise of the power of hearing,
we place ourselves where the groves are most melodi-
ous, or where the instruments are best toned, or where
the voices have most compass and variety ; and thus
we prepare to enjoy music. All this is natural and
necessary. And it is not equally so, if we would be
cheered by faith, to believe cheering truths? We
might as well roll our eyes in darkness, or fix them
upon a blank, and then doubt their visual power, as
judge of our faith whilst we abstain from trying to
believe the glad tidings of salvation. This will never
do at the sacrament, nor anywhere else that comfort
is needed. Wherever we come to God, we must
believe that He is the rewarder of them that diligently
seek Him. In no one duty, and at no ordinance, can
we be happy without believing the promises with

which it is connected, and of which it is the pledge. And we are as welcome to embrace them, as to obey it. Now, we never doubt our obligation to obey the laws of God; but the moment we look at them, we feel bound by their authority, and awed by their sanctions. So we ought to judge and feel. We are not, however, more bound to revere them, than we are welcome to believe the Gospel. The promises are just as free to our faith, as the commandments are binding on our conscience. Conscience, without the Law, would be an insufficient and unsafe guide; and Faith, without the promises, would be a miserable comforter, and a fruitless principle.

GEORGE PHILIP AND SON, PRINTERS, LONDON AND LIVERPOOL.

Printed in the United States
47007LVS00001B/25-48

9 781892 777461